Mapping Skills

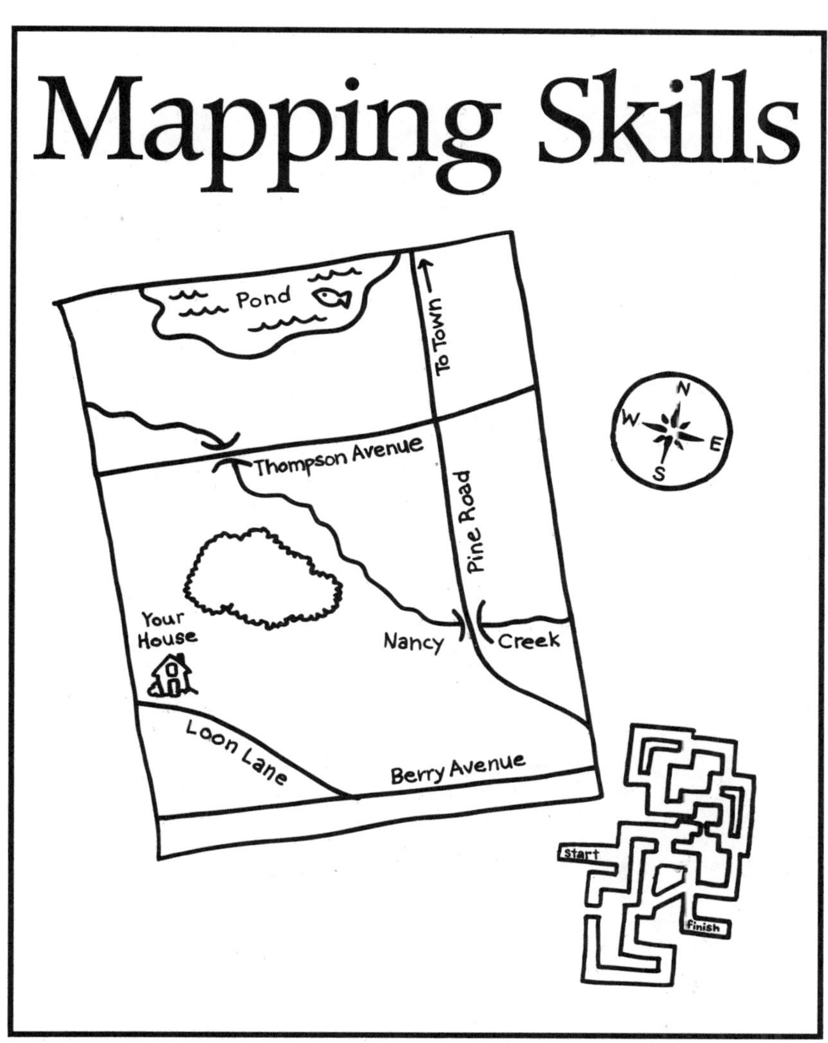

Mapping Skills

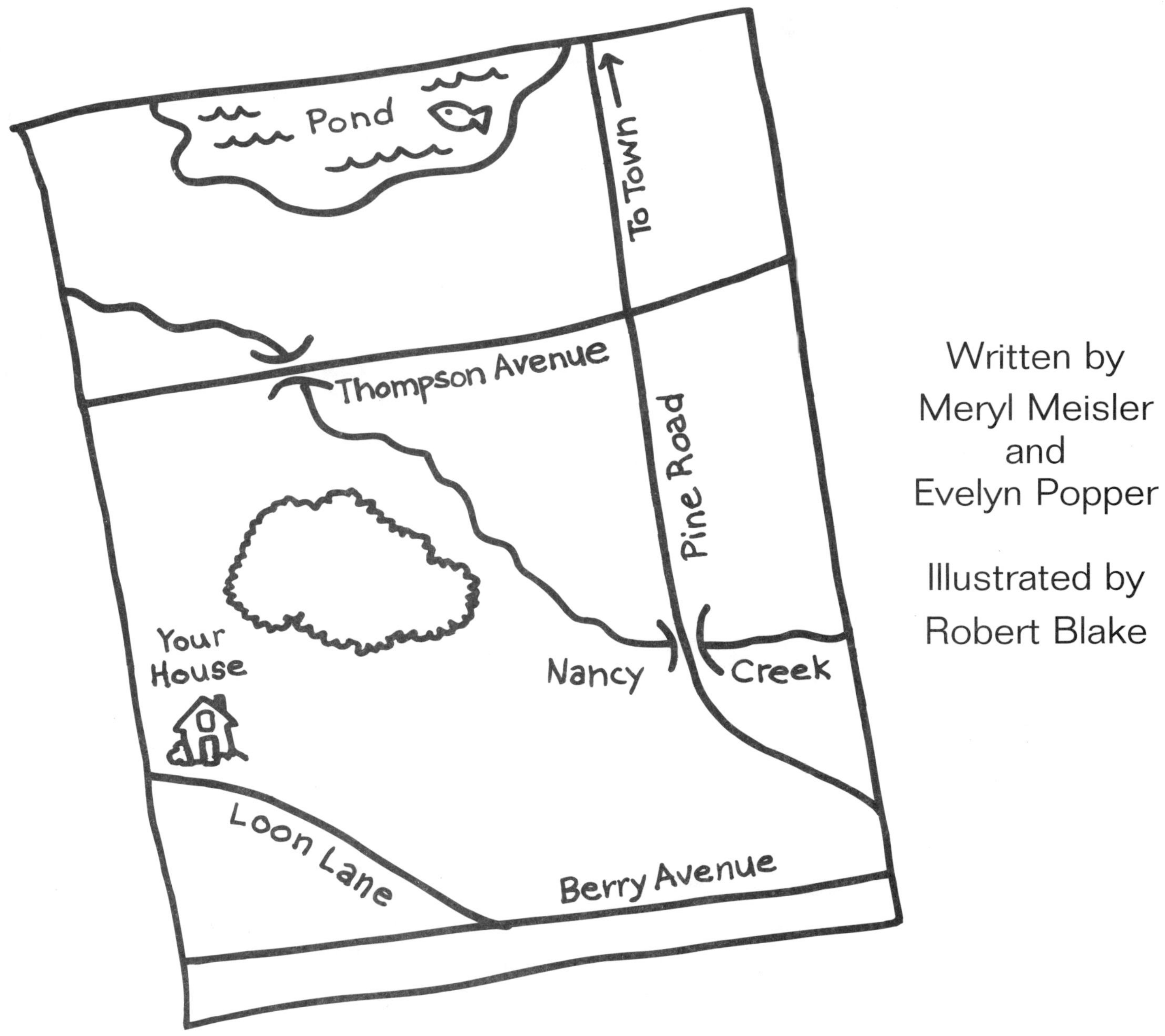

Written by
Meryl Meisler
and
Evelyn Popper

Illustrated by
Robert Blake

Newbridge Educational Publishing

Published in 1998 by Newbridge Educational Publishing, 333 East 38th Street, New York, NY 10016.

ISBN: 1-56784-711-0

10 9 8 7 6 5 4 3 2 1

Dear Teacher,

The wealth of maps and map-related activities in the MAPPING SKILLS book will provide your students with hours of fun and fascination. As they learn to read and use maps, they will be enhancing their reading and thinking abilities as well. Learning "map language" will improve their general language skills; figuring out latitude and longitude will call upon their knowledge of math. Most of all, becoming familiar with maps will enhance their knowledge of social studies, for maps can offer graphic pictures of significant historical events are invaluable aids in developing an understanding of the geography of the world.

Section one, Getting Ready, instructs children in map skills and terminology. Younger students can practice such basic skills as visually discriminating between lines in "Clowning Around" and between shapes and colors in "The Queen's Jewels." Connecting the numbers on "Walloon's Balloons" will promote number awareness. "Cymbal Symbols" will teach older students about map symbols, while "A Scale-y Ghost" will demonstrate the concept of scale. "In All Directions" introduces the compass rose. Other pages give practice in working with map keys, legends, and coordinates. Unscrambling "Little Map's Mixed-up Map Words," hopping down the "Stairway from the Sky," and playing "Map-Word Basketball" are pleasurable ways to learn map terminology.

In the second section, students will practice working with diagrams and graphs. They will discover how handy diagrams are when they find stadium seats for "Touchdown Time!" or examine the solar system in a "Swing Around the Sun." Creating a bar graph enables students to chart sales in "Dollars and Cakes." Maps of make-believe places supply hours of fun-filled discoveries as students use a bus route map while "Visiting Vampireville," color in some "Fantasy Islands," trace the route of "Claude Canary's Escape," and design a "Playground Plan."

In the third section, children will work with maps of cities, states, and provinces. By shading in spaces on a puzzle, they will "Find the Hidden State." Maps are good planning tools, as students discover when they plan a cycling group's "Rhode Island Road Trip." By identifying map outlines, they can straighten out some "States of Confusion" and figure out the names of several "Puzzling States." Working directly on maps, students draw delivery routes for "Corny's Nebraska Cornbread" and chart "Roads for Puerto Rico." In answering "Quebec Questions," they will learn about important industries. They'll learn how to decipher latitude and longitude when they plot the course for an adventure-filled "Cape Cod Cruise."

In section four students will use crayons to produce "Colorful Countries" and to create "Local Colors" on a map of the United States. Special puzzles and games in this section include "Short States," a crossword puzzle with abbreviations as clues; a TV quiz game, "Name That State!"; and an exciting, teacher-directed "Canadian Cities Game" that reviews map keys. This section includes a population map in "We, the People," a habitat map in "Animals at Home," and a weather map that students can create themselves in "Weather, Whether or Not."

In the final section, students use maps for a variety of purposes as they learn about countries around the world. A map of Europe aids in unscrambling a list of "Scrambled Countries," and a map of London allows students to plan "A Day in London" for a sightseer. Comparing two maps of Africa, children find the necessary information for planning an "African Journey." They will enjoy tracing the journey of the early Jamestown settlers in "Before the Pilgrims" and drawing the route of a traveling horror show, "The Tasmanian Devils," on a map of Australia.

Maps open up exciting pathways to the world and its wonders, and we believe this book will give you and your students the means and inspiration to explore the world again and again. Happy journeys!

Sincerely,

Stephanie Pliakas

Stephanie Pliakas
Editor

Mapping Skills

CONTENTS

Mapping Skills

CONTENTS

Name ____________________

CLOWNING AROUND

To read and understand maps, you need sharp eyes. Look carefully at this unfinished picture of a circus clown. Find the ten parts that are missing. Then, with a pencil, draw in the missing parts.

Name ______________________

THE QUEEN'S JEWELS

Queen Ruby Esmeralda has a marvelous collection of jewels. They come in these five shapes:

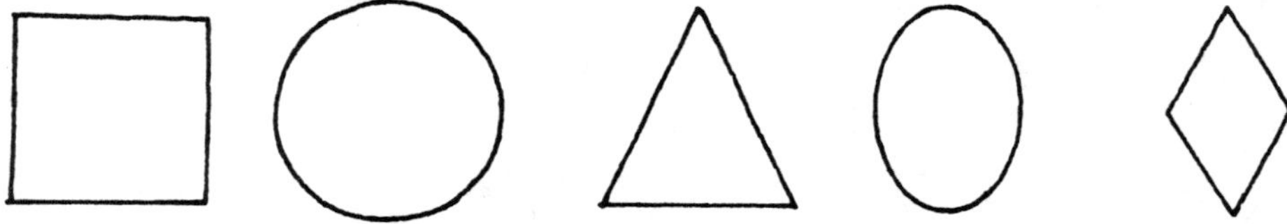

Each shape has its own color.

Look at the queen's jewels below. Then color them according to the directions in the box at the bottom of the page.

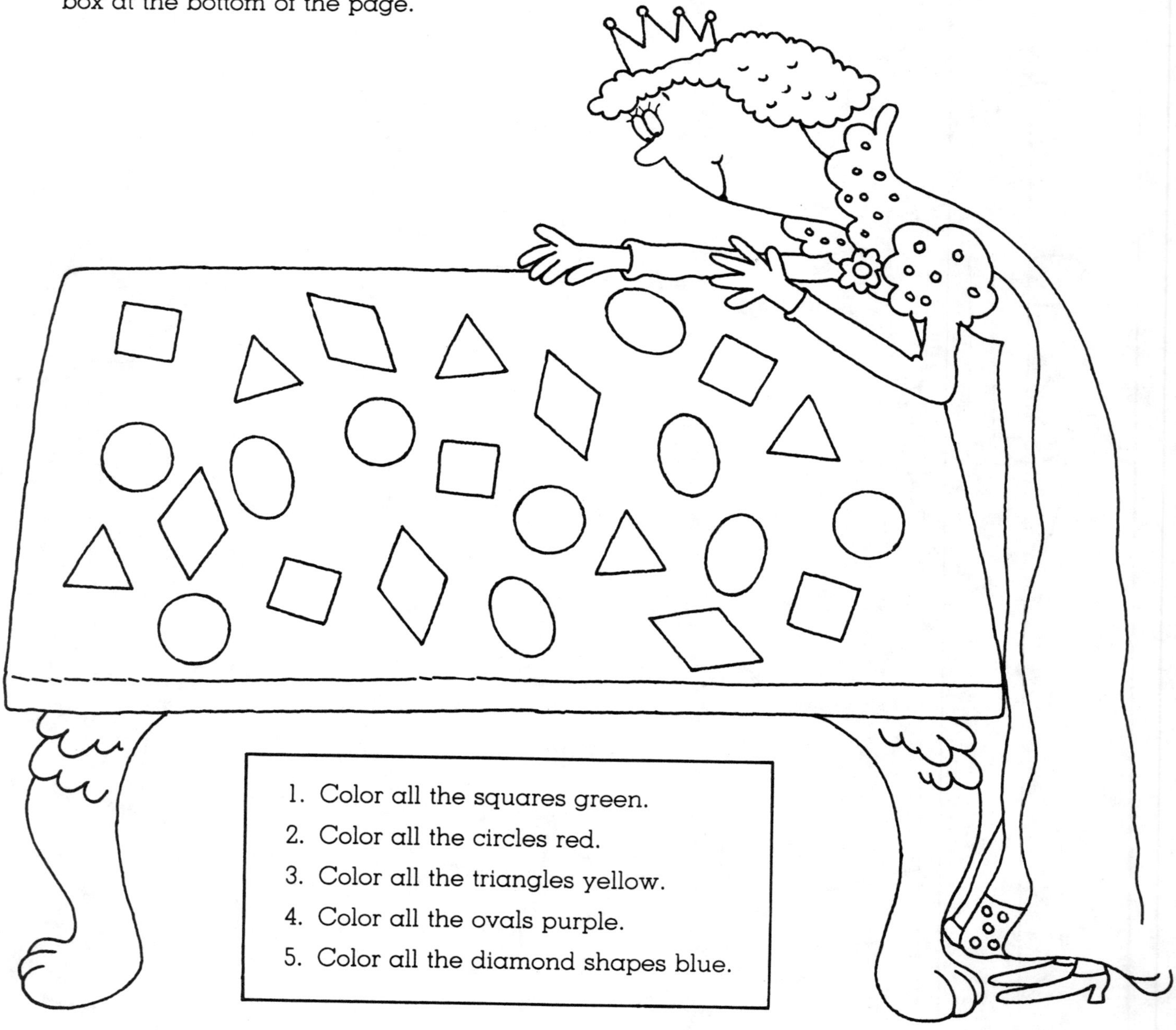

1. Color all the squares green.
2. Color all the circles red.
3. Color all the triangles yellow.
4. Color all the ovals purple.
5. Color all the diamond shapes blue.

Name ______________________________

WALLOON'S BALLOONS

Wally Walloon, who sells balloons, likes to keep his balloons in order. He ties all the even-numbered balloons to one side of his cart. He ties all the odd-numbered balloons to the other side.

Help Wally sort his balloons. With a red crayon, draw a line to connect all of the odd-numbered balloons in order, from 1 to 19. With a green crayon, draw a line to connect all of the even-numbered balloons in order, from 2 to 20.

Name ______________________

LITTLE MAP'S MIXED-UP MAP WORDS

While playing with his alphabet blocks, Little Map, the mapmaker's child, made some map words. But Little Map isn't old enough to put all the letters in the right order, so you will have to help him.

Look at each set of blocks and read each definition below it. Each set contains letters that spell out a word used in making and reading maps. The first three letters of each word are in the correct order. Unscramble the rest of the letters. Then write each correct word in the spaces provided.

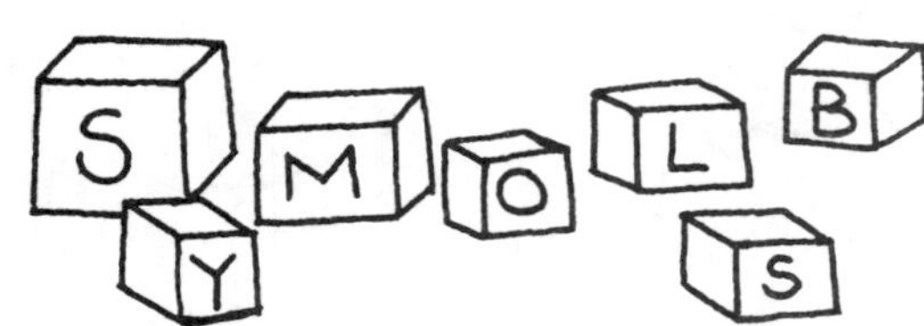

Little pictures used on some maps to show the locations of cities, roads, bridges, airports, and so on

1. __ __ __ __ __ __ __

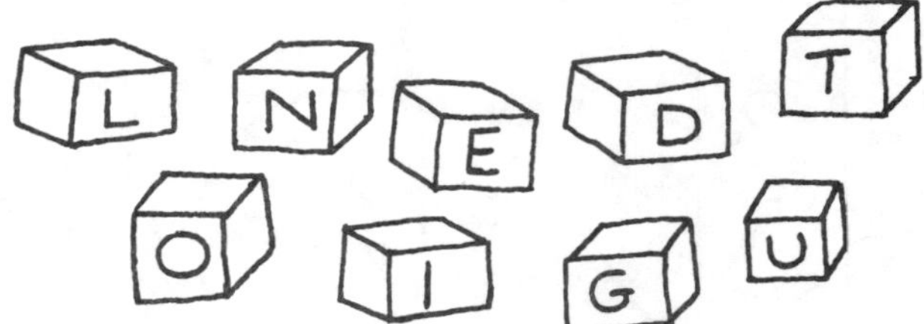

Lines running vertically—north and south—used to locate points on a map grid

4. __ __ __ __ __ __ __ __ __

Lines running horizontally—east and west—used to locate points on a map grid

2. __ __ __ __ __ __ __ __

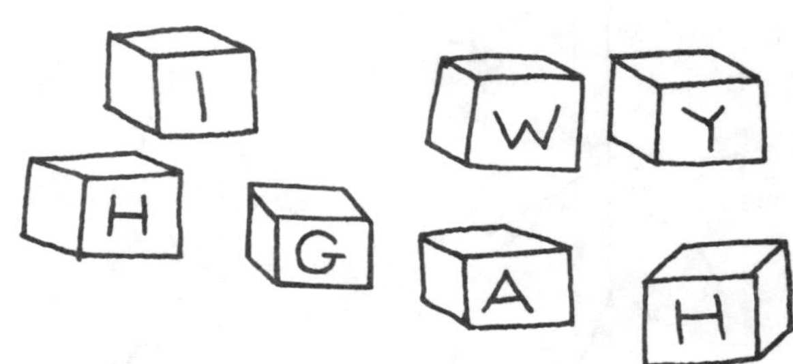

A kind of road

5. __ __ __ __ __ __ __

A direction

3. __ __ __ __ __ __ __ __ __

Name ______________________

STAIRWAY FROM THE SKY

To make a map of an area, mapmakers have to know what the area looks like. Can you guess what they sometimes use to help them? To find out, hop down the steps of this stairway from the sky.

First, read the definitions below and the words listed in the Word Box. Write the correct words in the squares. Then, on the lines at the bottom of the page, write only the letters in the shaded squares, starting at the top step and ending at the bottom step. Then read the sentence to learn what a mapmaker uses.

...... The opposite of closed

...... Chocolate- ________ cookies

...... The opposite of short

...... Something bright that twinkles in the sky

...... Where some astronauts have landed

...... The opposite of pretty

...... Short for *graduate*

...... Sleeps during the day

...... Chimpanzees and gorillas

...... To cut in small pieces

Word Box	
chip	chop
naps	apes
moon	grad
star	ugly
open	long

A ___ ___ ___ ___ ___ ___ ___ ___ ___ ___ can be used to help make a map.

Name ______________________

MAP-WORD MAZE

The word *coordinates* is an important map word. To find out what it means, work your way through this maze. There are four definitions attached to the maze, but only the correct definition can be reached. Start at the center and, with your pencil, draw a path to the correct meaning of *coordinates*.

Name ___________________________

DON'T WAIT—ABBREVIATE!

To save space, words on maps are often abbreviated, or made shorter. Read the map abbreviations on the crates below. Then read the whole words on the suitcase at the bottom of the page. Match each word with its abbreviation. Write the whole word on the line under each abbreviation. Use an atlas, if necessary.

Name ______________________________

CYMBAL SYMBOLS

A symbol is painted on each cymbal in the Silly Symbol Cymbal Band. But only five of these symbols are likely to appear on maps. Can you find the five map symbols? They're hidden in the scrambled words below. Unscramble each map symbol word and write it correctly on the line provided. Then write the letter of the symbol next to its matching word.

NMUOTANI

1. ______________________ ____

DRAALIRO

3. ______________________ ____

ILO EWLL

2. ______________________ ____

ILATPCA

4. ______________________ ____

GIBRED

5. ______________________ ____

Name ______________________________

COUSIN MADELINE'S MAP LEGEND

Cousin Madeline Mapmaker is adding a map legend to a map she has just made. Cousin Madeline is very good at drawing symbols, but she's not so good at remembering what they mean. You can help her. Look at each symbol. Read the three choices next to it. Circle the letter of the meaning you think is correct.

	Symbol	Meaning		
1.		a. state capital	b. bridge	c. skateboard
2.		a. mountain	b. pocket comb	c. railroad
3.		a. national capital	b. factory	c. movie star
4.		a. mountain	b. caterpillar	c. airport
5.	0 1 MILE	a. compass rose	b. ruler	c. map scale
6.	N W E S	a. pinwheel	b. railroad	c. compass rose
7.		a. puddle	b. lake	c. small rug
8.		a. slice of pie	b. oil well	c. contour lines
9.		a. saw	b. shark teeth	c. factory
10.		a. tepee	b. bridge	c. airport

Name ______________________________

IN ALL DIRECTIONS

On most maps, there's a design called a *compass rose* that shows direction. Uncle Mac Mapmaker always draws the compass rose on all the Mapmaker family maps. Unfortunately, Uncle Mac has a poor sense of direction. He knows which way is north, but after that he's lost. Finish Uncle Mac's job for him. Look at the compass rose below. One compass point—N for North—has already been filled in. Follow the rules in the box to write seven other compass points in the correct places on the lines provided.

1. Use these abbreviations:
   N = North; S = South; E = East; W = West; NE = Northeast; NW = Northwest; SE = Southeast; SW = Southwest.
2. When north is at the top, west is on your left, east is on your right, and south is on the bottom.
3. Northwest is between north and west, southwest is between south and west, and so on.

Name ____________________

A SCALE-Y GHOST

Maps have to be much smaller than the areas they stand for. But they still have to show the correct distance between one place and another. To do this, maps are drawn to *scale*. Drawing a picture will help you understand how scale works.

Look at this drawing of a ghost. It is covered by a grid of boxes, each marked by a letter-number combination. The same grid, only larger, covers the space below.

With your pencil, draw the same thing in each square below as appears in the smaller square with the same number and letter. Continue with each square until you have drawn a large picture of a ghost. Square B4 has already been done for you.

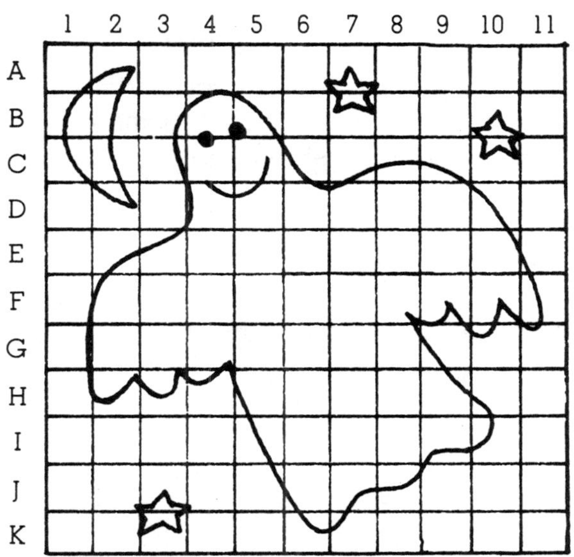

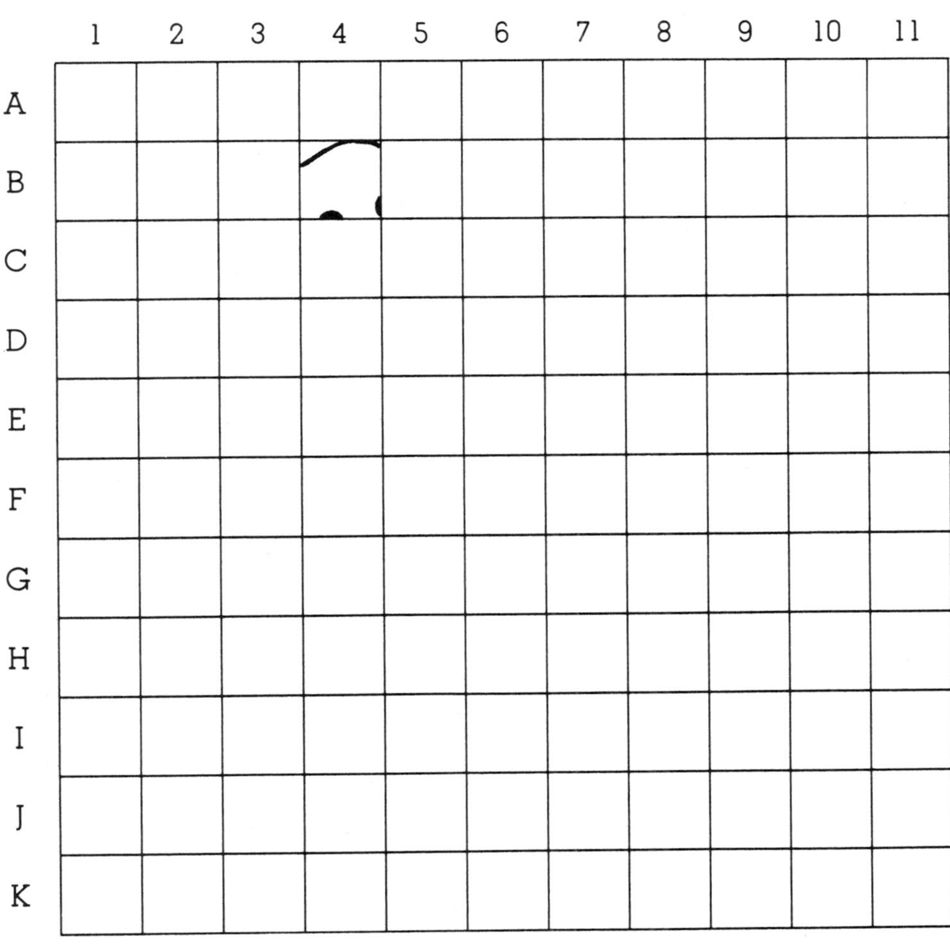

Name ________________

A KEY TO KUMQUAT

An *atlas* is a book of maps. In most atlases, you will find letters and numbers around each map. These are called the *map key*. It is used to find places on a map. First read the instructions on using a map key. Then look at the map of the make-believe country of Kumquat. Notice the six towns on this map. Using the instructions, find the town closest to each map key letter and number below and write it on the line provided.

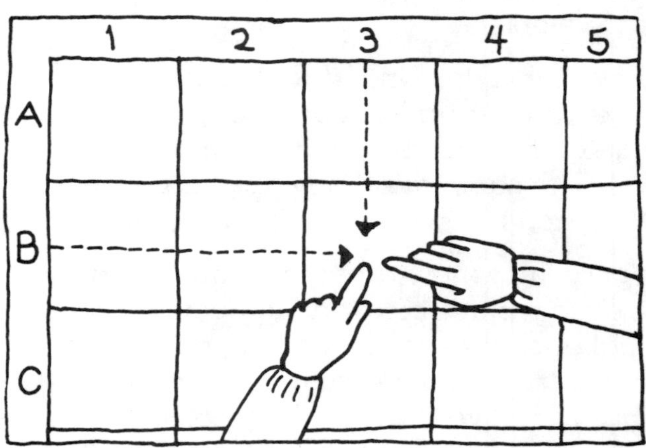

How to Use a Map Key:
Let's say you want to find "Berryburg," and the listing in the atlas reads:

Berryburg—B3

On the map, you would put a finger of one hand on the letter *B*, and a finger of the other hand on the number 3. Then you would move your fingers along the map until they meet. Somewhere near this point you will see Berryburg.

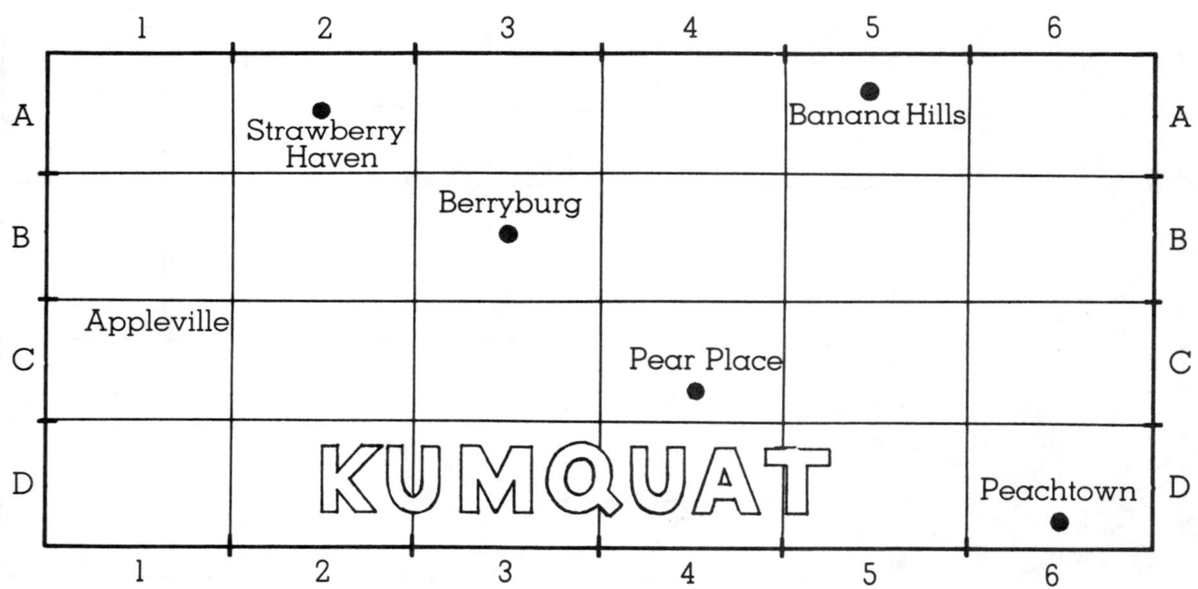

1. C1 ________________
2. D6 ________________
3. A2 ________________
4. A5 ________________
5. C4 ________________

Name ____________________

ALL AROUND LATITUDE

Read the following passage and examine the illustration. Use the information to complete the statements at the bottom of the page. Circle the letter of each correct answer.

Lines of *latitude* (lat.), also called parallels, are imaginary lines drawn on maps and globes to help us find places. Lines of latitude run horizontally, circling the globe east and west. These lines are numbered in degrees (°). Zero degree latitude (0°) marks the *equator*, an imaginary line running around the middle of the earth. Lines of latitude go from zero to 90° in either direction, north and south. Latitude above the equator is called north latitude (N). Latitude below the equator is called south latitude (S).

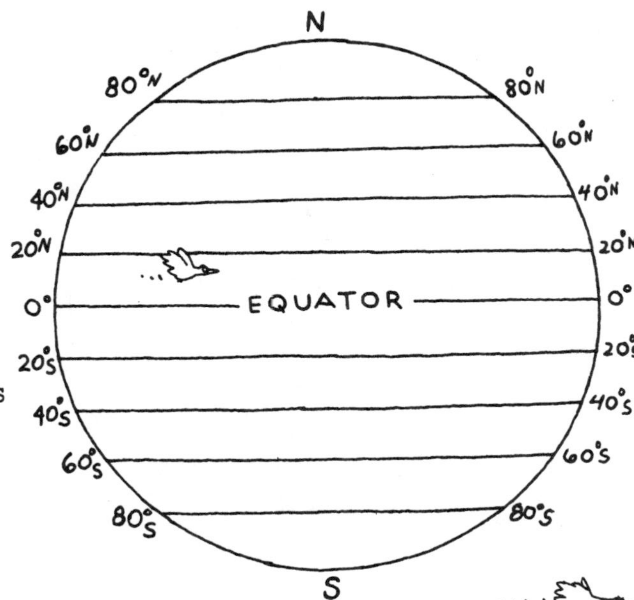

1. On maps and globes, lines of latitude run

   a. north and south   b. east and west   c. south and east

2. Latitude lines are also known as

   a. parallels   b. contours   c. meridians

3. Lines of latitude are numbered in units called

   a. segments   b. meters   c. degrees

4. Below the equator latitude is called

   a. polar latitude   b. south latitude   c. north latitude

5. The abbreviation for the word *latitude* is

   a. ltd.   b. ltde.   c. lat.

Name ______________________

UP-AND-DOWN LONGITUDE

Read the following passage and examine the illustration. Use the information to complete the statements at the bottom of the page. Circle the letter of each correct answer.

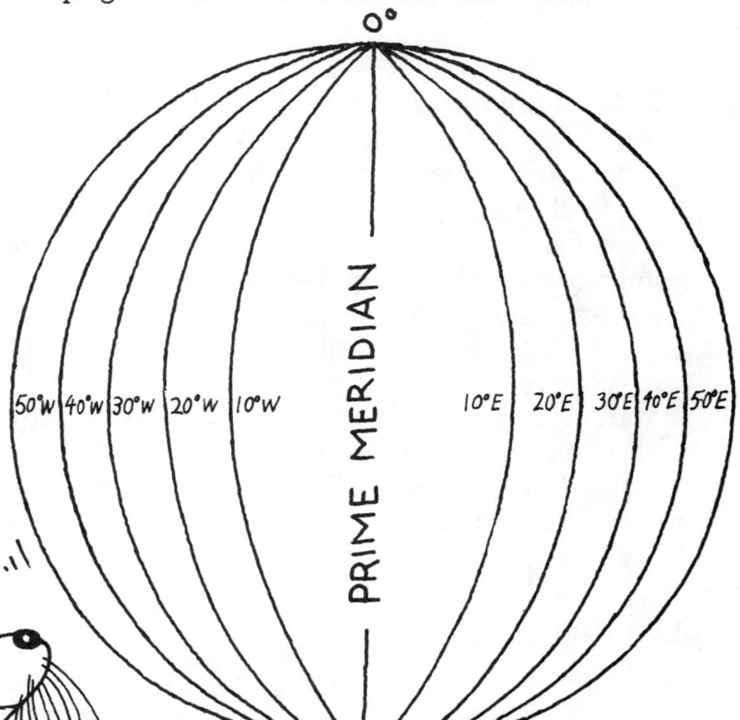

Lines of *longitude* (long.), also called meridians, are imaginary lines drawn on maps and globes to help us find places. Lines of longitude run up and down, circling the globe north and south. These lines are numbered in degrees (°). Zero degree longitude (0°) marks the *prime meridian*, an imaginary line going through Greenwich, England. Lines of longitude go east and west to 180° from this point.

Longitude left of the prime meridian is called west longitude (W). Longitude right of the prime meridian is called east longitude (E).

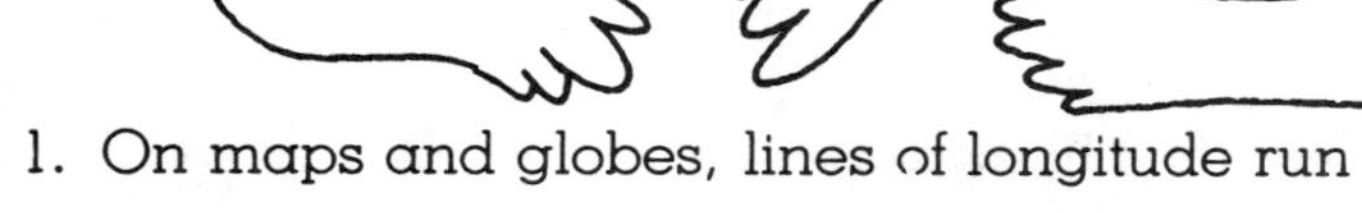

1. On maps and globes, lines of longitude run

   a. north and south b. east and west c. side to side

2. Longitude lines are also know as

   a. parallels b. meridians c. polar lines

3. The symbol for "degree" is

   a. D b. # c. °

4. The imaginary line that goes through Greenwich, England, is called the

   a. vertical b. zero azimuth c. prime meridian

5. The abbreviation for the word *longitude* is

   a. long. b. lgde. c. Lg.

Name ______________________

WORDS IN THE BASKET

Read the words in the basket. Look up any words you don't know in a dictionary. Then read the sentences below. Complete each one by choosing the correct word or words from the basket and writing it on the line provided.

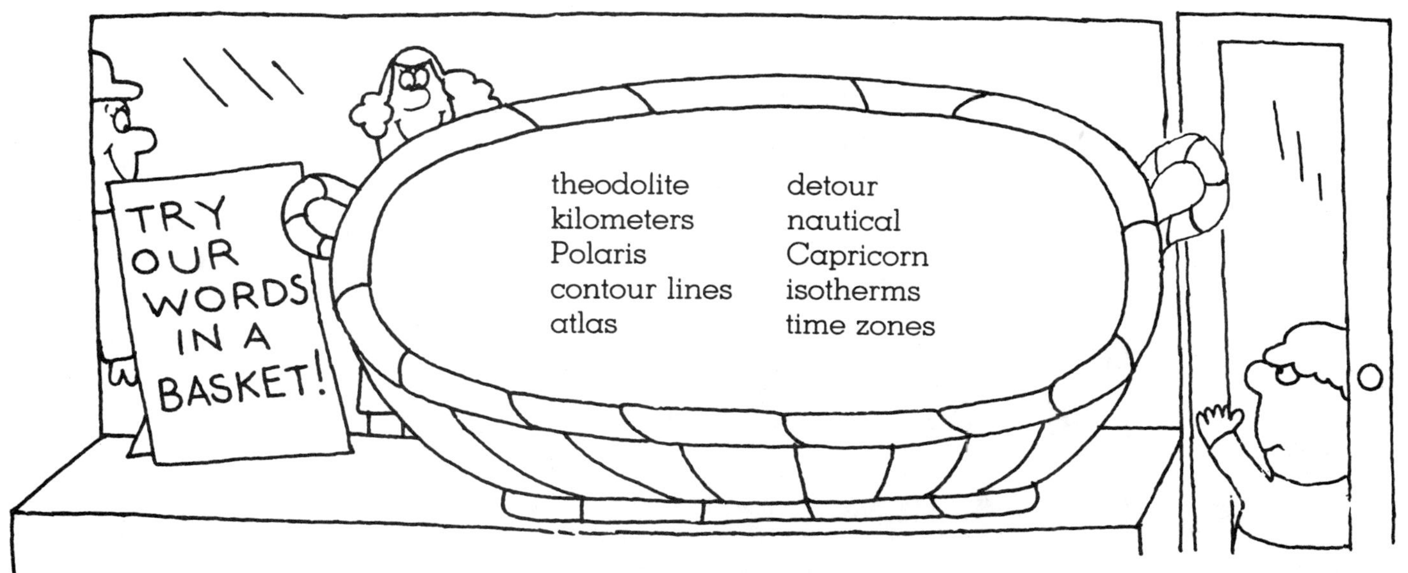

1. Although the ship was caught in a storm, the captain found his way by using his ______________ chart.
2. Before announcing the temperatures across the country, the TV reporter checked the ______________ on her weather map.
3. For her class report, Jenny looked in her ______________ to find a map of Venezuela.
4. To tell direction at night, try to find the North Star, also called ______________ .
5. The four ______________ in the continental United States are Pacific, mountain, central, and eastern.
6. To measure angles on the ground, a surveyor uses a ______________ .
7. Scales at the bottom of maps are usually given in both miles and ______________ .
8. The torrid zone lies between the tropic of Cancer and the tropic of ______________ .
9. On some flat maps, it's possible to tell the height of hills and mountains by studying ______________ .
10. Mr. Shiftgear learned about the highway ______________ by referring to his road map.

Name ____________________

DOES IT COMPUTE?

Chip Microchip is having trouble with his new computer. Sometimes the facts on his computer screen are correct, but sometimes they are not! Read the statements on the screen below. Look up each underlined word in a dictionary. Then draw a check mark (✓) on the line above *T* if the statement is true. Draw a check mark (✓) on the line above *F* if the answer is false.

Name ______________________

ARROW WORDS

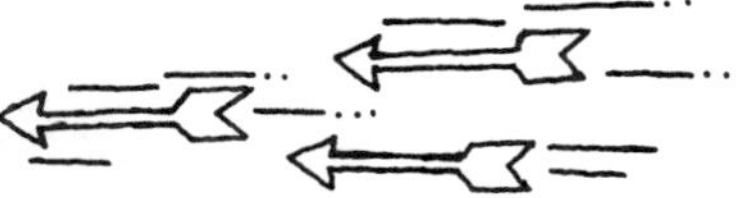

Written inside the arrows below are words that have to do with maps and mapmaking. For each arrow word, there are three targets containing definitions. But only one definition is correct. Read each arrow word. Then choose the definition that is correct and write its letter on the line below each arrow. Use a dictionary, if necessary.

isthmus

a. a large body of water surrounded by woods

b. a short word for Christmas

c. a narrow strip of land connecting two larger land areas

1. ______

meridian

a. on maps, another word for a line of longitude

b. a large swampy area in the South

c. a new rock group

2. ______

elevation

a. a moving room that carries people up

b. the height above level ground of a structure, hill, or mountain

c. on maps, the width of a river

3. ______

isobars

a. frozen desserts on sticks

b. lines on weather maps connecting all points that have the same barometer readings

c. large sheets of ice left by glaciers

4. ______

surveyor

a. an expert who measures land and water areas for mapmaking

b. a fancy telescope used for studying the stars

c. someone who digs for gold

5. ______

Name ______________________

MAP-WORD BASKETBALL

Read the words written on the basketballs. Each describes a geographic area found on maps. Read the definitions of these words on the basketball hoops. Decide which definition fits each word. Write its letter on the line below each basketball. Use a dictionary, if necessary.

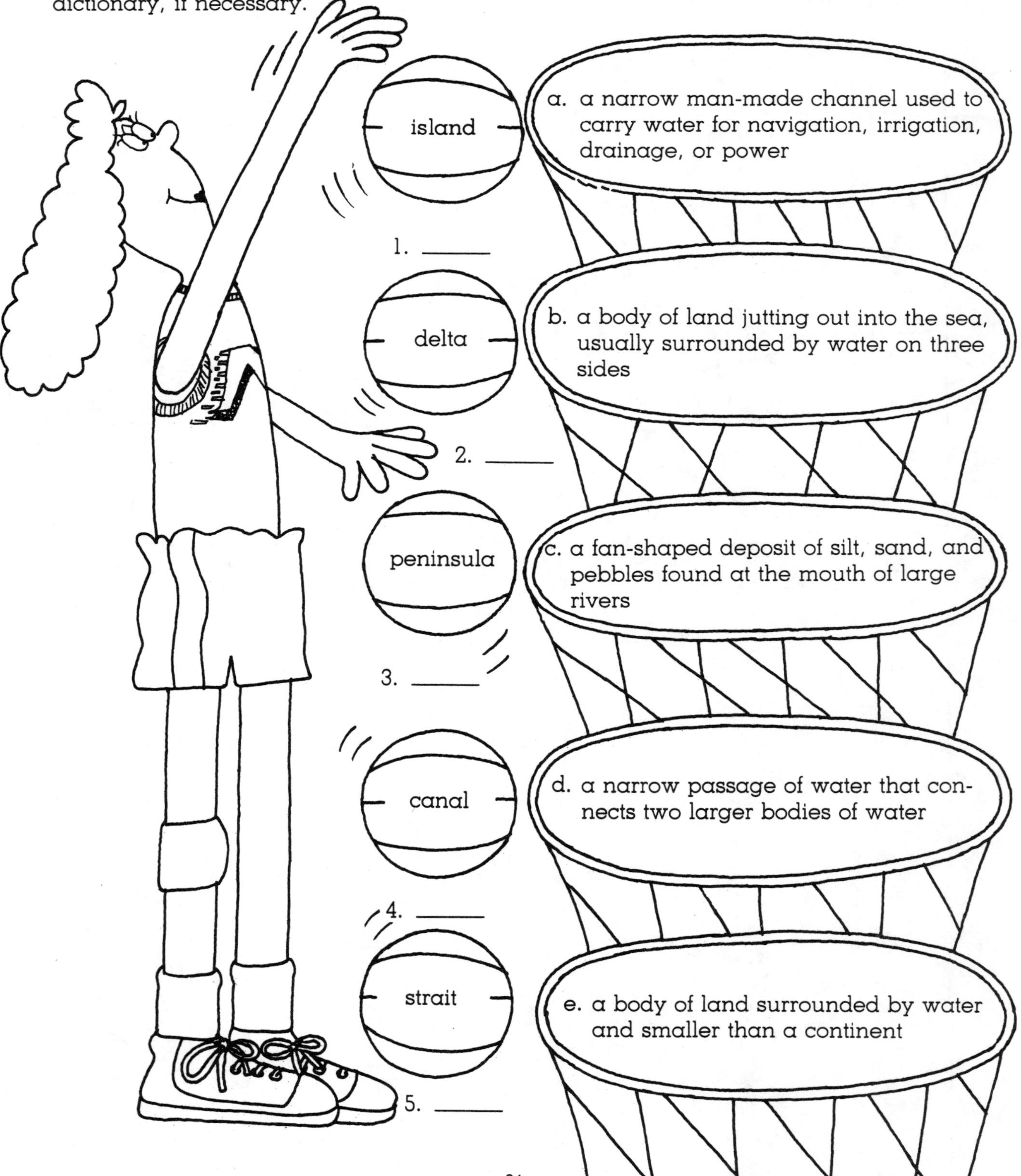

Answer Sheet for *Getting Ready*—Section 1

Clowning Around—page 7

The Queen's Jewels—page 8

Walloon's Balloons—page 9

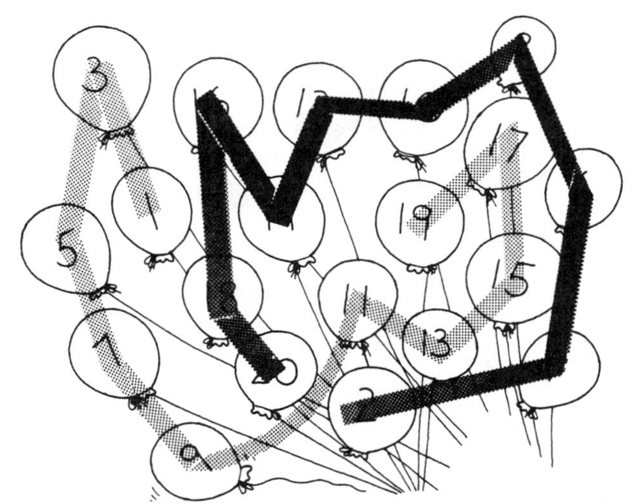

Little Map's Mixed-up Map Words—page 10

1. symbols
2. latitude
3. southeast
4. longitude
5. highway

Stairway from the Sky—page 11

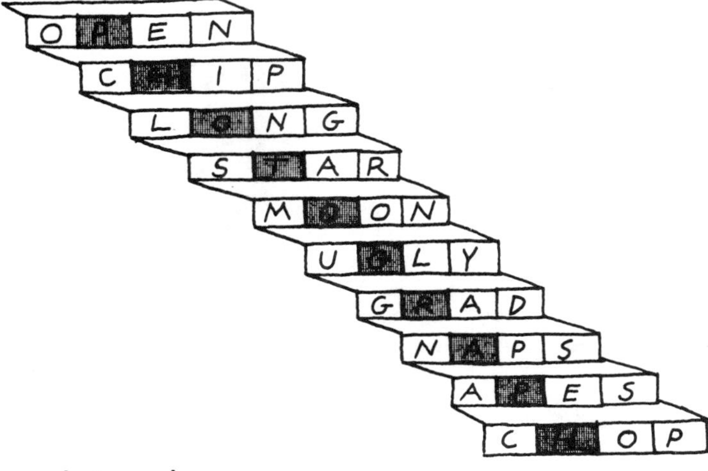

photograph

Map-Word Maze—page 12

Answer Sheet for *Getting Ready*—Section 1

Don't Wait—Abbreviate!—page 13

cont. continent	rep. republic
dist. district	Can. Canada
U.S. United States	mts. mountains
pen. peninsula	prov. province
pop. population	isl. island

Cymbal Symbols—page 14

1. mountain—A
2. oil well—C
3. railroad—F
4. capital—H
5. bridge—I

Cousin Madeline's Map Legend—page 15

1. b
2. c
3. a
4. a
5. c
6. c
7. b
8. b
9. c
10. c

In All Directions—page 16

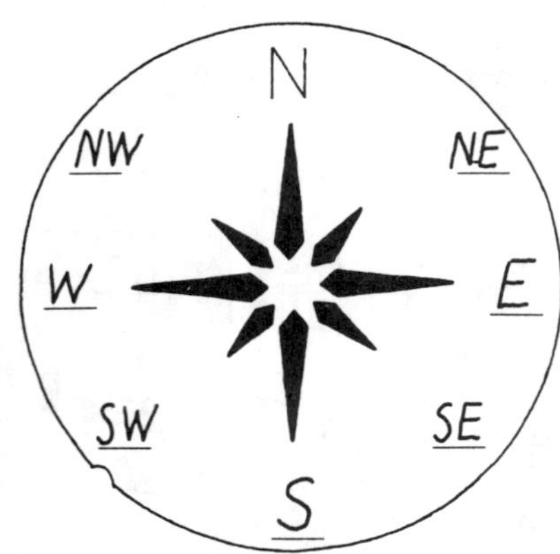

A Scale-y Ghost—page 17

Check students' drawings against the drawing on page 17.

A Key to Kumquat—page 18

1. Appleville
2. Peachtown
3. Strawberry Haven
4. Banana Hills
5. Pear Place

All Around Latitude—page 19

1. b
2. a
3. c
4. b
5. c

Up-and-Down Longitude—page 20

1. a
2. b
3. c
4. c
5. a

Words in the Basket—page 21

1. nautical
2. isotherms
3. atlas
4. Polaris
5. time zones
6. theodolite
7. kilometers
8. Capricorn
9. contour lines
10. detour

Does It Compute?—page 22

1. T
2. F
3. F
4. T
5. F

Arrow Words—page 23

1. c
2. a
3. b
4. b
5. a

Map-Word Basketball—page 24

1. e
2. c
3. b
4. a
5. d

Name ______________________

FOOT MAP FUN

Maps give us information about size and shape and tell us where things are. To make a map of your foot, place this page faceup on the floor. Now take off your right shoe but leave your sock on. Place your foot in the box below. With a pencil or crayon, carefully trace the outline of your foot. Draw an arrow pointing to your heel and label it "My Heel." Next draw an arrow to your big toe and label it "My Big Toe."

Congratulations! You've just made a map of your foot! Put your shoe back on.

A MAP OF MY RIGHT FOOT

Name ______________________

WHO'S NEW AT THE ZOO?

A new shipment of creatures has just arrived at Storytime Zoo. Each one must be put in its new home. Look at the map at the bottom of this page. It shows where each creature belongs. Write the letter of each creature on the line in its proper place.

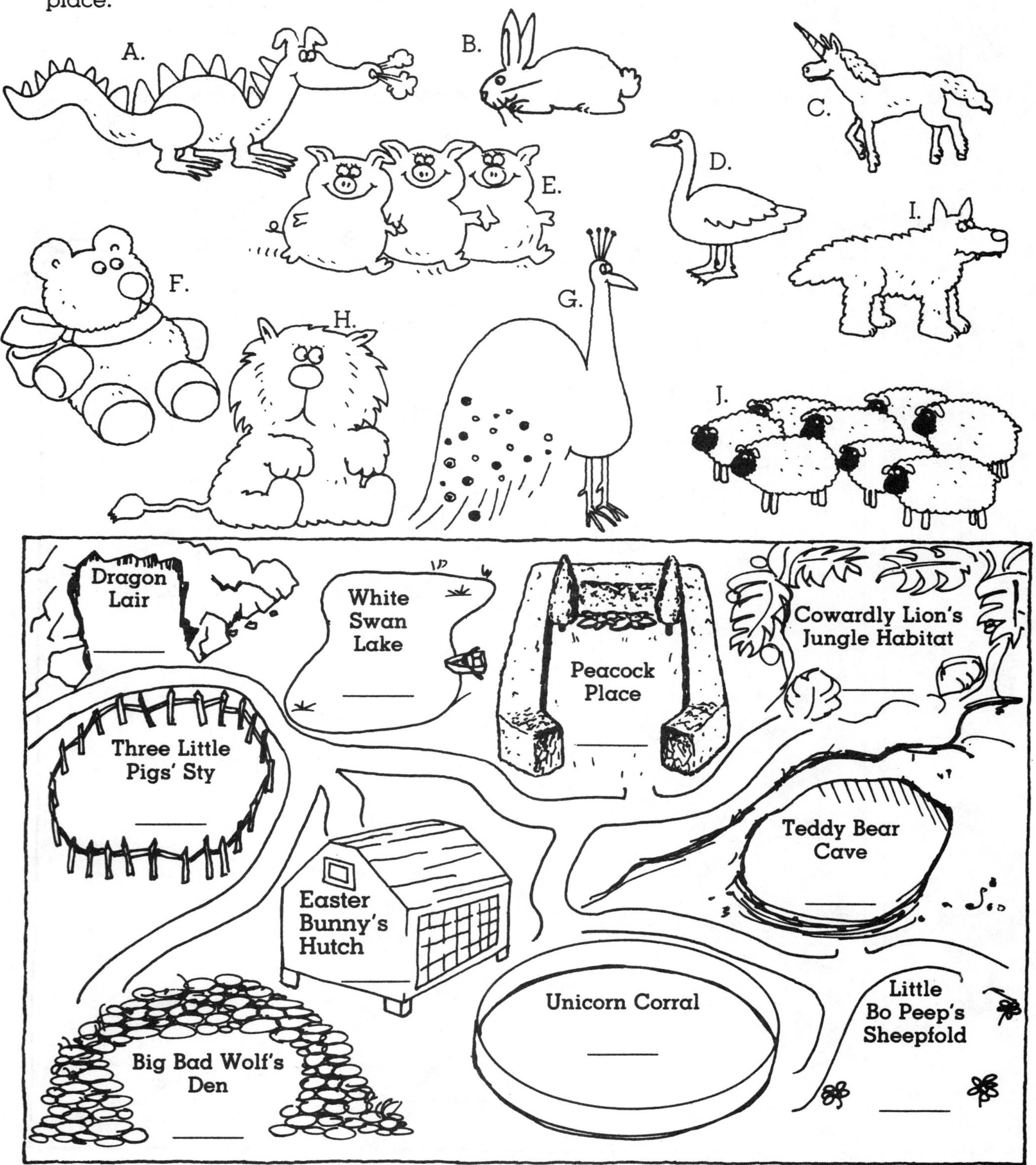

Name ____________________

FANTASY ISLANDS

Map colors are very useful. They help us to see shapes and to tell the difference between land and water areas. Look at the make-believe islands below. With your crayons, color each one according to the following directions:

1. Color the first island green.
2. Color the fourth island brown.
3. Color island 8 yellow.
4. Color island 6 red.
5. Color the second island purple.
6. Color the ninth island orange.
7. Color the last island pink.
8. Color the island between island 2 and island 4 black.
9. Color the island between island 6 and island 8 blue.
10. Which island is left? Write the number here. ____________ Color this island tan.

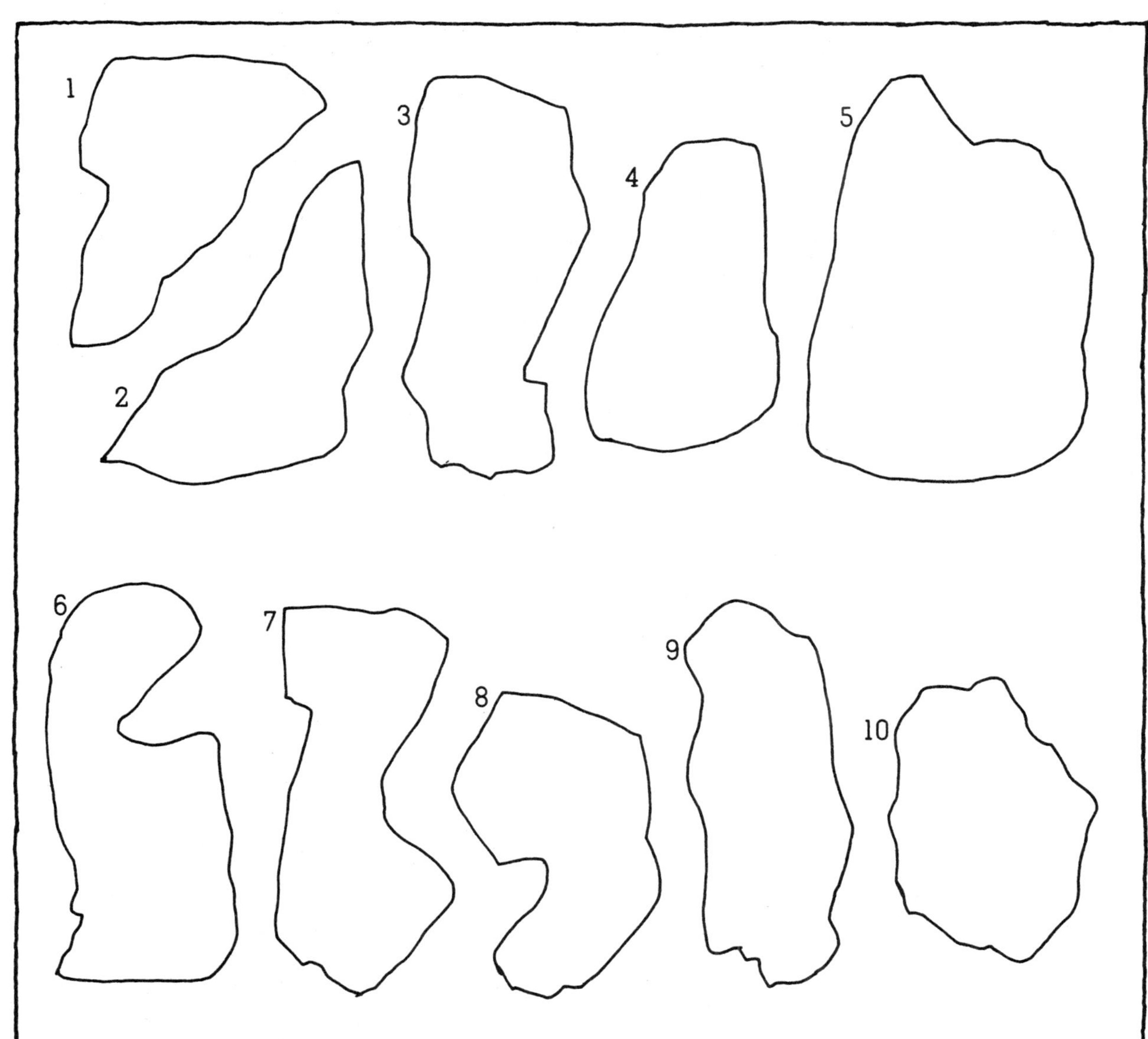

Name ______________________

CLAUDE CANARY'S ESCAPE

Robin Byrd kept Claude Canary in a cage in her house. But now Claude has escaped from his cage and flown away from the Byrd house. Read the directions below and look at the map and compass rose. Then, with your pencil, trace Claude's route to the spot where he is hiding now.

MAPLE ISLAND

FERN ISLAND

ROCKY FALLS

N
W
E
S

Claude's Escape Route

1. From the house Claude flew to the pointed rock.
2. Then he flew northwest to the big weeping willow tree.
3. From there he flew southwest to the old wooden dock.
4. Next, Claude flew southeast to Maple Island.
5. From Maple Island, he flew south to the rowboat.
6. Then he flew northeast to Fern Island.
7. From there he flew southeast to the huge boulder.
8. Next he flew east to Rocky Falls.
9. From Rocky Falls Claude flew northwest to the sunken tree.
10. Finally, Claude flew northeast to the old boathouse. He's there right now.

Name ______________________

TOUCHDOWN TIME!

Here is a seating diagram of a football stadium. The seats are arranged in sections. Each section is marked with a letter of the alphabet. Look at the sections, the field, and the entrance gates. Then complete the true-false statements below.

Which of these statements is true? Which is false? If a statement is correct, draw a check mark (✔) on the line above T (true). If it is not correct, check the line over F (false).

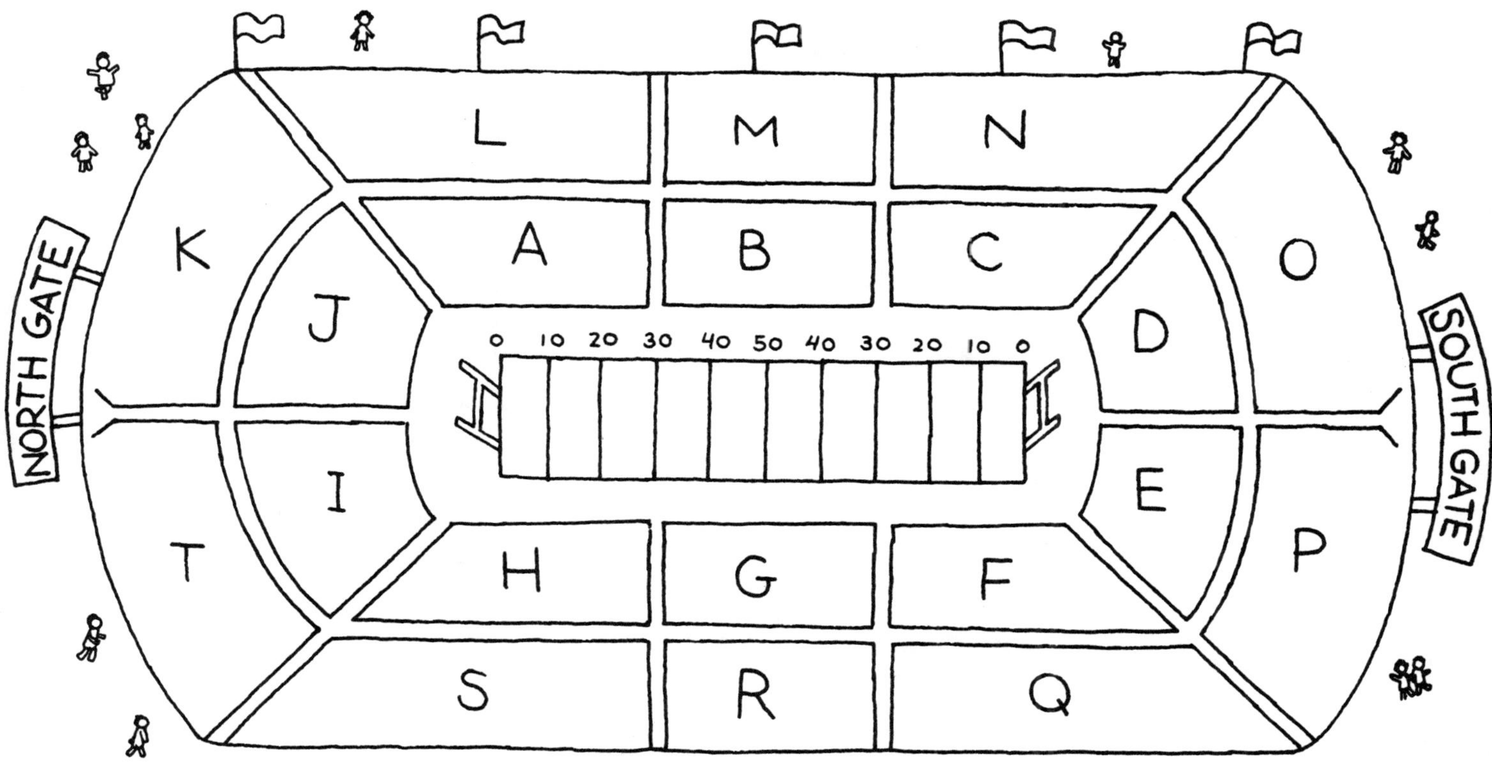

1. If you want good seats on the 50-yard line, you should be in section B or section G.
   ____ T ____ F
2. If you want to sit as close to the football field as possible, you should be in section M, S, or P.
   ____ T ____ F
3. Fans in sections D and E are very close to the north goalposts.
   ____ T ____ F
4. The middle of section F is even with the southern 30-yard line.
   ____ T ____ F
5. Sections T, K, J, and I are all at the north end of the field.
   ____ T ____ F

Name ______________________________

DELIVER THE MAIL

Flora Fauna is the new mail carrier for the town of Dandelion. She needs help delivering the five pieces of mail below. Can you lend a hand? Read the address on each envelope and look at the neighborhood map. Then write the letter of each envelope on the matching house on the map to show where it should be delivered.

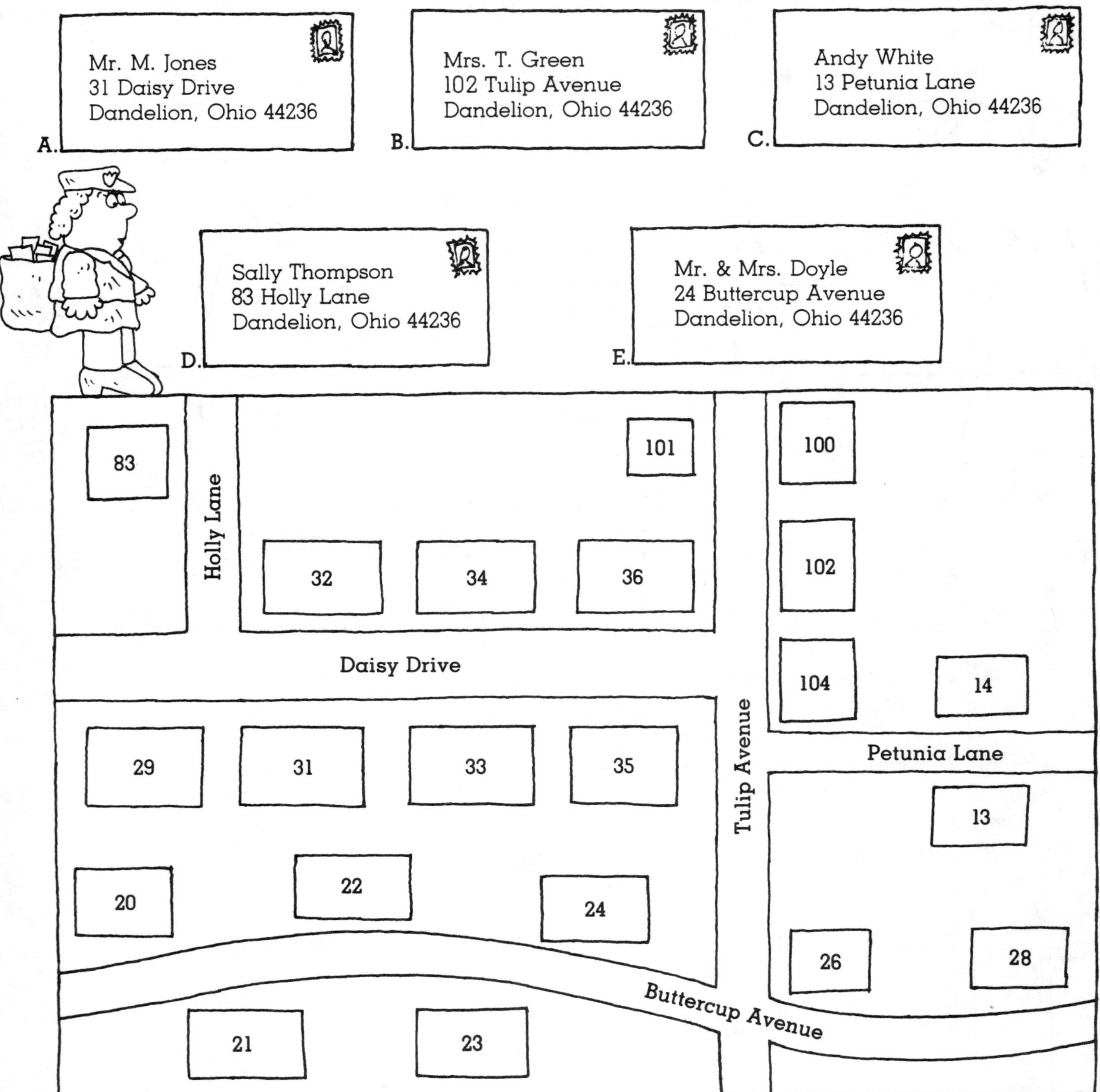

Name ______________________

BIKING TO HENRY'S HOUSE

Your new school friend, Henry, has invited you to his house for the afternoon. You are going by bike, but don't know the route, so Henry has given you a map. Look at the map and read the questions below. Write your answers on the lines provided.

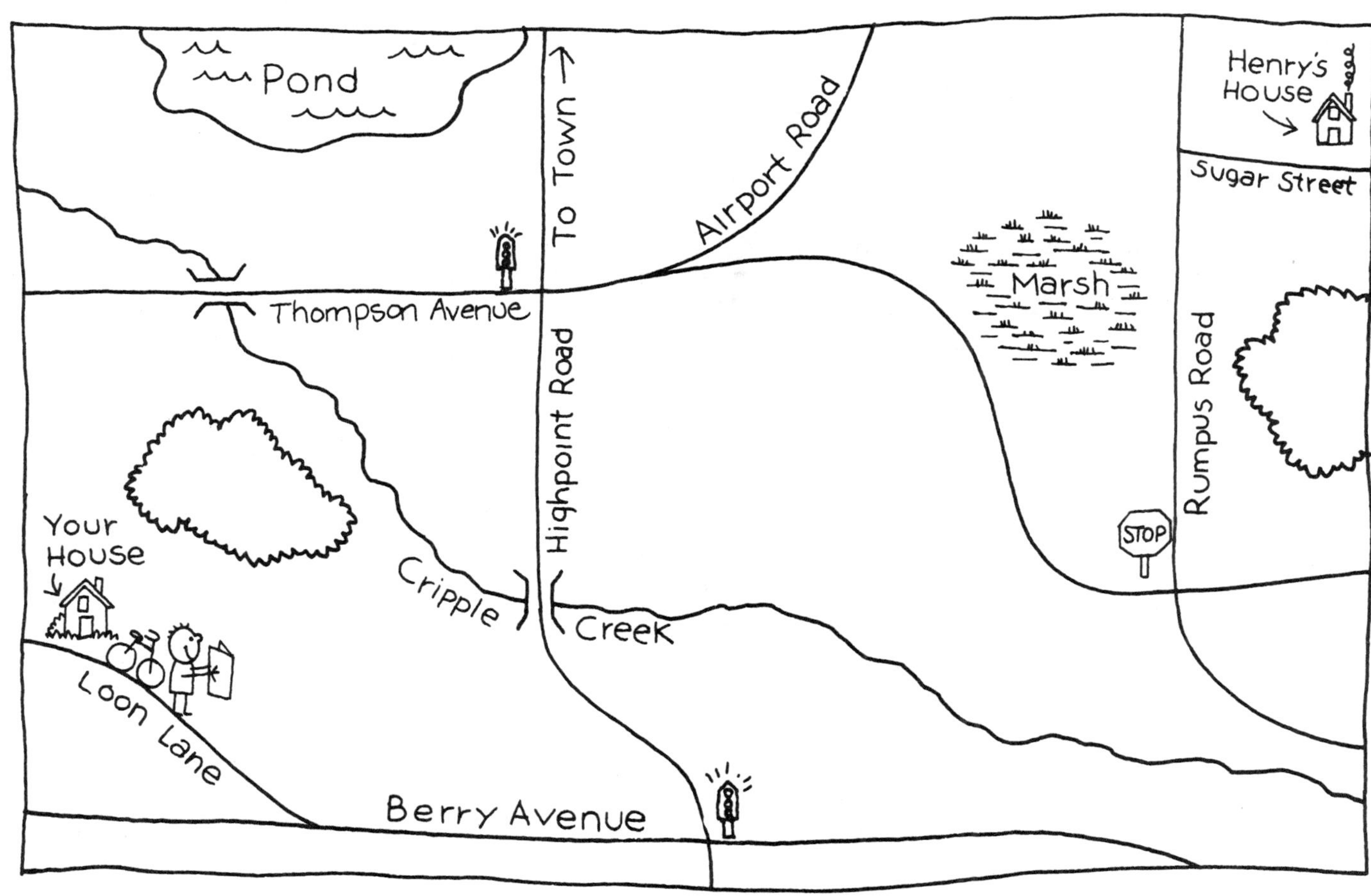

1. The lane where your house stands is called ______________________.
2. From there, what avenue will you ride along? ______________________
3. At the first traffic light, which way will you turn, right or left? ______________________
4. How will you get across Cripple Creek? ______________________
5. At the second traffic light, which way will you turn? ______________________
6. Where the road divides, will you go right or left? ______________________
7. Thompson Avenue curves sharply. Why? ______________________
8. At the stop sign, which way will you go, right or left? ______________________
9. What is the name of the road you will be on? ______________________
10. At what street will you next turn right? ______________________

Name ______________________________

PLEASE BE SEATED!

Your school is having a rock concert, and you are in charge of the seating. The diagram below shows all the seats in the auditorium. Each seat can be located by its number and by the letter of the row it's in. Study the diagram and read the questions below. Write your answers on the lines provided or shade in the diagram as directed.

M	109	107	105	103	101	1	2	3	4	5	6	7	8	102	104	106	108	110	M
L	109	107	105	103	101	1	2	3	4	5	6	7	8	102	104	106	108	110	L
K	109	107	105	103	101	1	2	spotlights and video camera			6	7	8	102	104	106	108	110	K
J	109	107	105	103	101	1	2	3	4	5	6	7	8	102	104	106	108	110	J
H	109	107	105	103	101	1	2	3	4	5	6	7	8	102	104	106	108	110	H
G	109	107	105	103	101	1	2	3	4	5	6	7	8	102	104	106	108	110	G
F	109	107	105	103	101	1	2	3	4	5	6	7	8	102	104	106	108	110	F
E	109	107	105	103	101	1	2	3	4	5	6	7	8	102	104	106	108	110	E
D	109	107	105	103	101	1	2	3	4	5	6	7	8	102	104	106	108	110	D
C	109	107	105	103	101	1	2	3	4	5	6	7	8	102	104	106	108	110	C
B	109	107	105	103	101	1	2	3	4	5	6	7	8	102	104	106	108	110	B
A	109	107	105	103	101	1	2	3	4	5	6	7	8	102	104	106	108	110	A

stage

1. The concert committee has invited the principal and his wife to have seats in the front row center. Which seats (row and numbers) will you assign them?

   ______ ______

2. A girl in a wheelchair needs a seat on the aisle, about halfway back. Which seat will you assign her, G5, F8, or B1?

   ______

3. Your homeroom teacher and her husband are in row F, seats 3 and 4. Find these seats. With a pencil, shade them in on the diagram.
4. Your parents and two of their friends have bought tickets for row D, seats 102, 104, 106, and 108. Find these seats on the diagram and shade them in.
5. A man sitting in row L, seat 5, is complaining about his seat. What do you think his reason might be? ______________________________

   ____

SWING AROUND THE SUN

Name________________

Solar means "having to do with the sun." This diagram of the solar system shows our sun and the paths of the planets that orbit, or revolve, around it. Look at the diagram and read the questions below it. Write your answers on the lines provided.

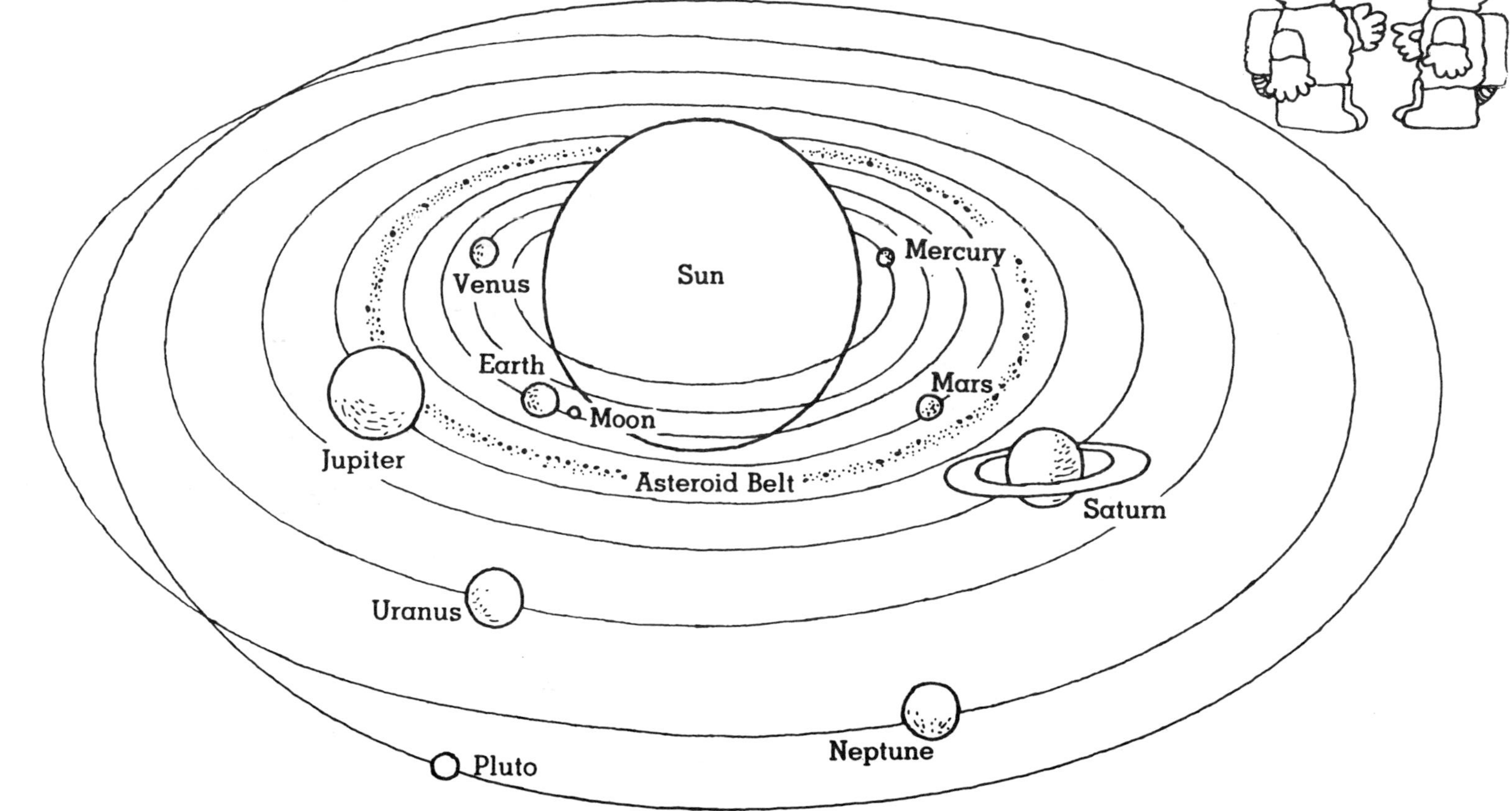

1. The planet that orbits closest to the sun is ____________ .
2. The planet that orbits farthest from the sun is ____________ .
3. ____________ is the sixth closest planet to the sun.
4. Planet Earth's orbit is between the orbits of the planets ____________ and ____________ .
5. The Asteroid Belt is situated between the orbits of the planets ____________ and ____________ .

Name ______________________

PLAYGROUND PLAN

Congratulations! You have just been elected Parks Director of your town! Now your job is to map out a fine new playground. First look at these symbols for playground equipment:

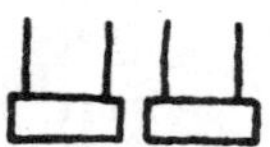
swings

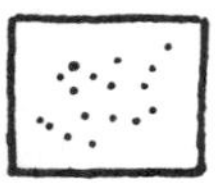
sandbox

seesaw

slide

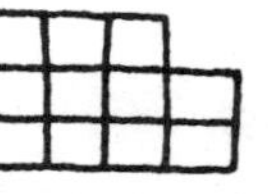
jungle gym

benches

Keep the following rules in mind:

1. Benches should be placed around the sides of the playground.
2. Sandboxes and jungle gyms should be placed away from swings and slides.
3. Show enough seesaws and swings for at least 12 children to use at one time.

Then decide how many pieces of each kind of equipment you will have and where each piece will go. Draw the symbols in the space below.

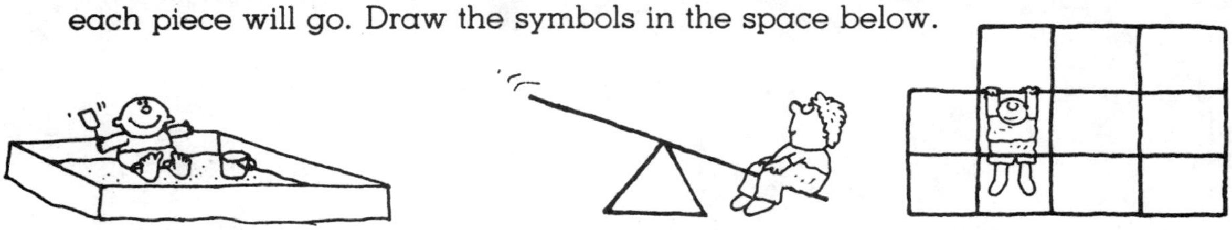

Name ______________________________

VIEW FROM THE TOP

Aunt Mavis Mapmaker has taken an aerial photograph of the coastal area near her town. Now she is using the photograph to make a map of the area. You can help Aunt Mavis with her work. Notice the objects in Aunt Mavis's photograph. Then look at the symbols for these objects in the box on the right. Draw each of these symbols in its correct place on Aunt Mavis's map.

photograph

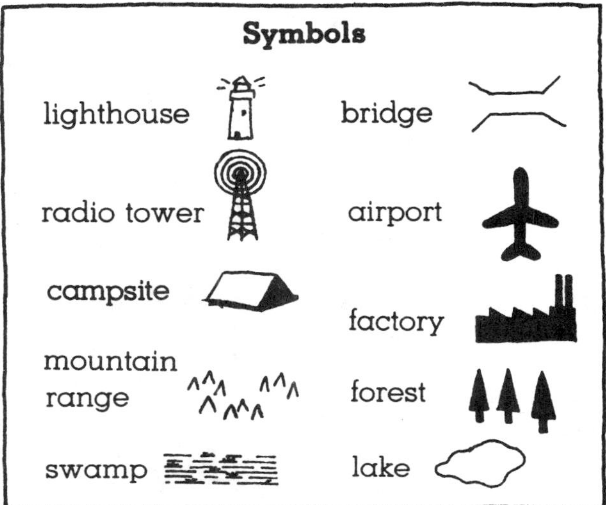

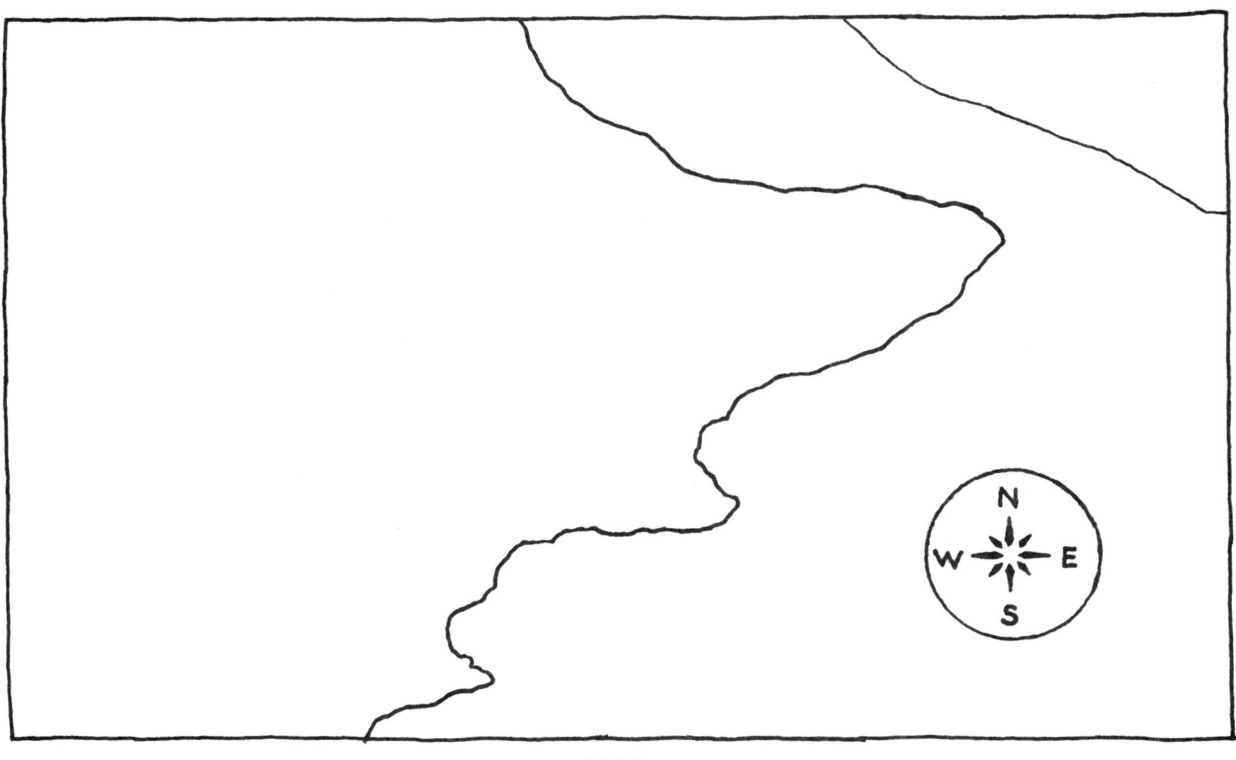

map

Name ________________________

OH NO, MORE SNOW!

Like maps, graphs give a lot of information quickly in the form of a picture. The graph below shows the amount of snow that fell on the make-believe town of Iglooville during 1984. Notice that the vertical lines show the months of the year and the horizontal lines show the amount of snowfall in inches. Use information from the graph to answer the questions below. Write your answers on the lines provided.

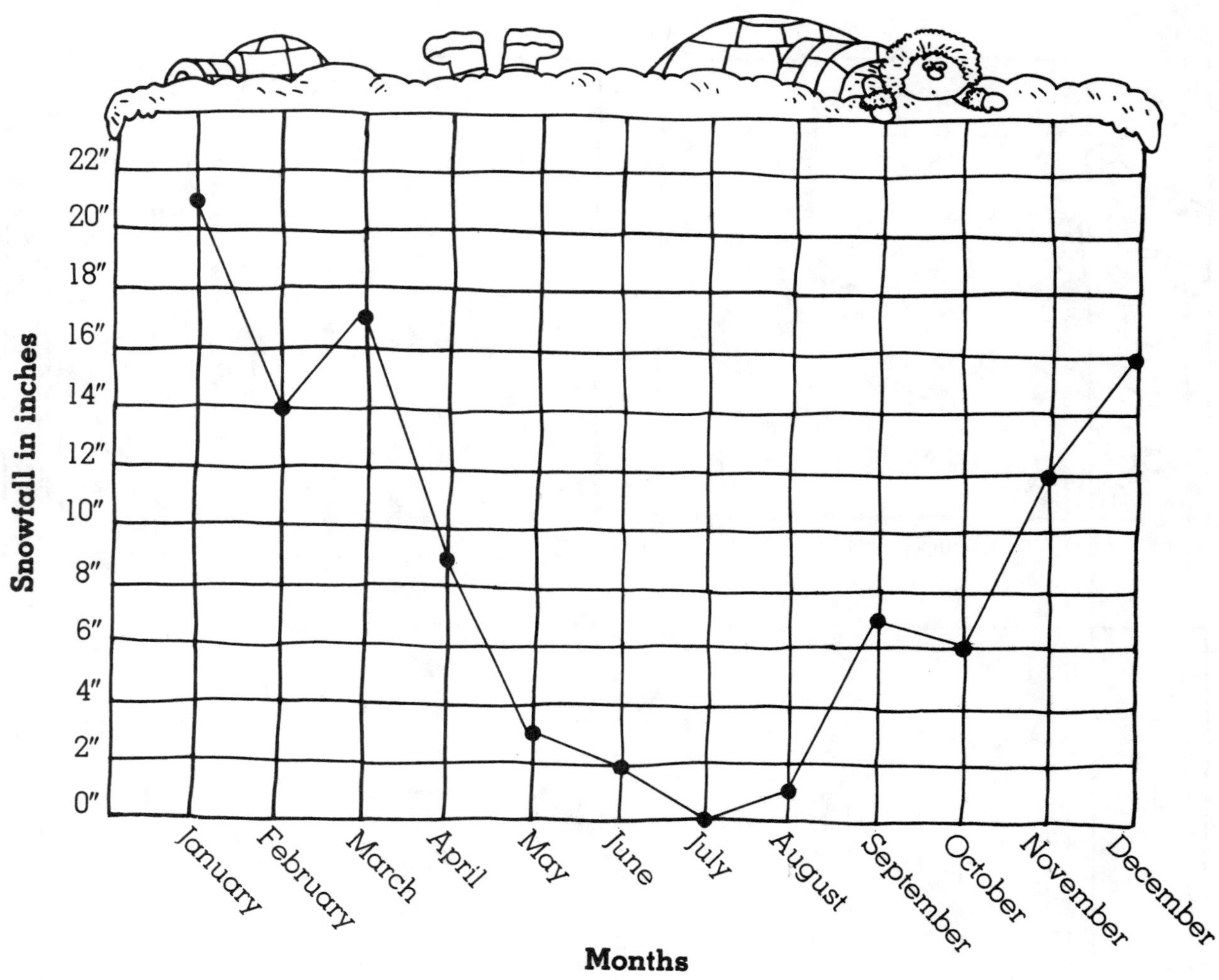

1. In which month did the greatest amount of snow fall in Iglooville? ____________
2. How many inches of snow fell at that time? ____________
3. How many inches of snow fell in May? ____________ October? ____________ August? ____________
4. Which two months had the least snow of all? ____________ and ____________
5. When did more snow fall—in February or in March? ____________ How many more inches fell? ____________

Name ____________________

DOLLARS AND CAKES

A *bar graph* uses bars to show information. The bar graph on the right, for example, shows the number of Wackadoos the Wacky Wackadoo Company sold during the first four months of 1985. To find out how many Wackadoos were sold in February, first find the bar labeled February. Then find the number at the left that is on the same line as the bar reaches. The answer is 25,000.

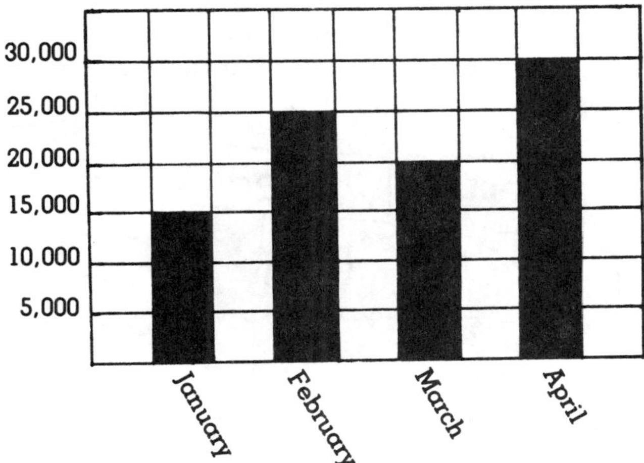

Employees of the Wacky Wackadoo Company hold a cake sale every month to raise money for the company basketball team, the Doowacks. With your help, they will be able to see at a glance exactly how much money they earned, month-by-month. In the box below are the figures for last year's cake-sale earnings. Use them to draw in the bars on the graph form at the bottom of the page. Then use information from your graph to complete page 40.

Earnings from Cake Sales

January $20, February $35, March $40, April $25, May $10, June $15, July $20, August $40, September $50, October $35, November $45, December $55

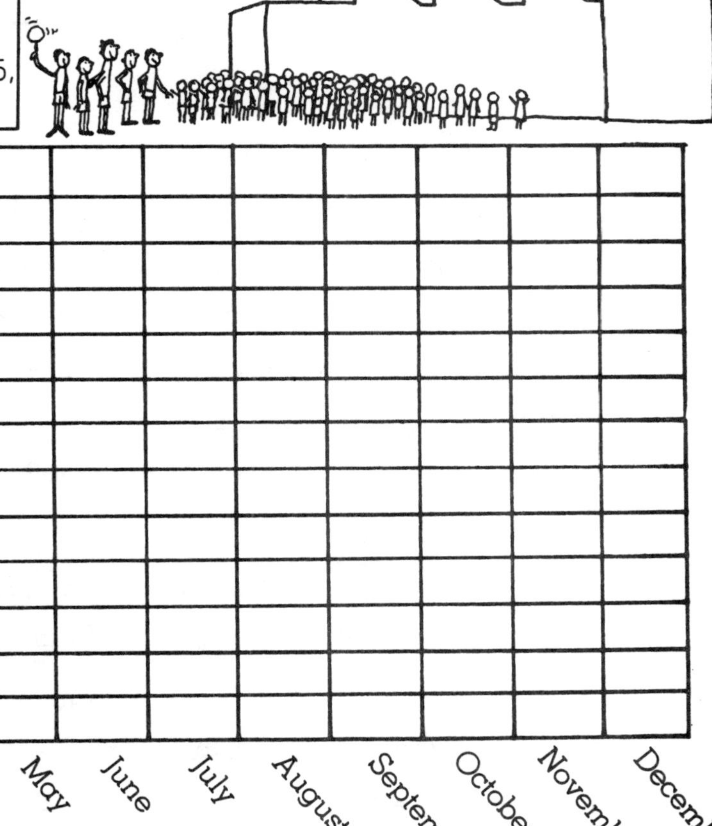

Name ______________________________

DOLLARS AND CAKES

Complete the bar graph on page 39. Then use information from it to answer the questions below. Write your answers on the lines provided. Use another piece of paper to show your work.

1. a. In which month was the most money earned? ______________________
   b. How much money was earned in this month? ______________________
2. a. In which month was the least money earned? ______________________
   b. How much money was earned in this month? ______________________
3. a. In which six-month period was the most money earned, January to June or July to December? ______________________
   b. How much money was earned altogether during this period? ______________________
4. a. From March to April, how much did earnings decrease? ______________________
   b. How much did earnings increase from August to September? ______________________
5. a. What was the total amount of money earned for the year? ______________________
   b. What was the average amount of money earned each month? (Divide the previous answer by 12.) ______________________

Name ____________________

ON THE ROAD AGAIN

Cal and Sal work for the Highway Department of Cayoose County. Today they are putting up road signs. You can help them. Look at the road signs below. Read what each one means. Use this information to complete page 42.

Intersection

Road on Right Ahead

Winding Road

Traffic Circle

Road Merges from Left

Name ______________________________

ON THE ROAD AGAIN

Look at the road signs on page 41 and read what each one means. Then look at the Cayoose County road map below. Notice that it shows an empty space next to each spot where Cal and Sal have to put a road sign. Decide which sign belongs in each space. Then cut out each sign and paste it in the correct space.

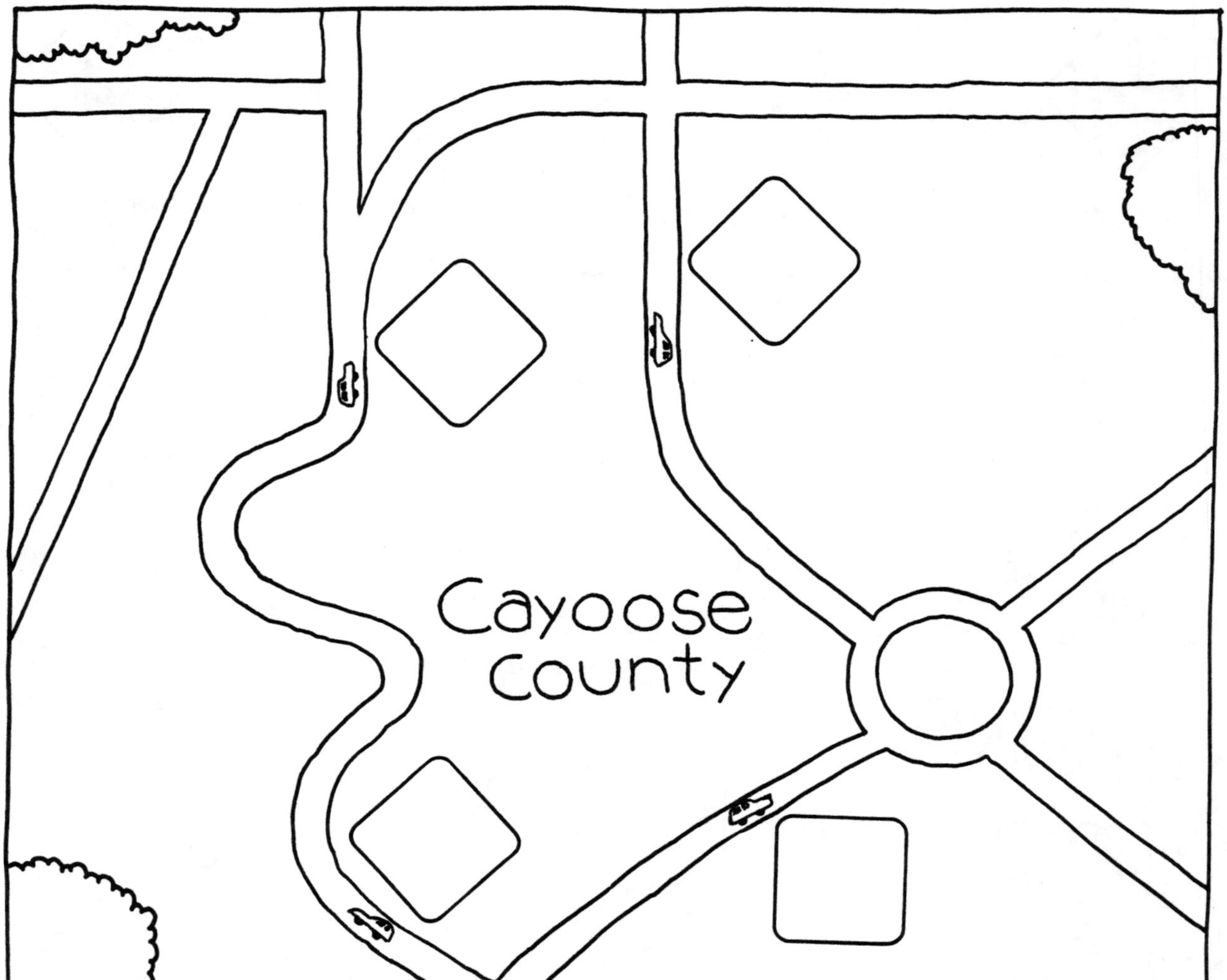

Cayoose County

VISITING VAMPIREVILLE

Name ______________________

The Batwing Bus Company plans the bus routes in Vampireville. The map below shows the three main bus routes of the downtown area. Study the map and the bus route key at the bottom of the page. Use information from them to complete page 44.

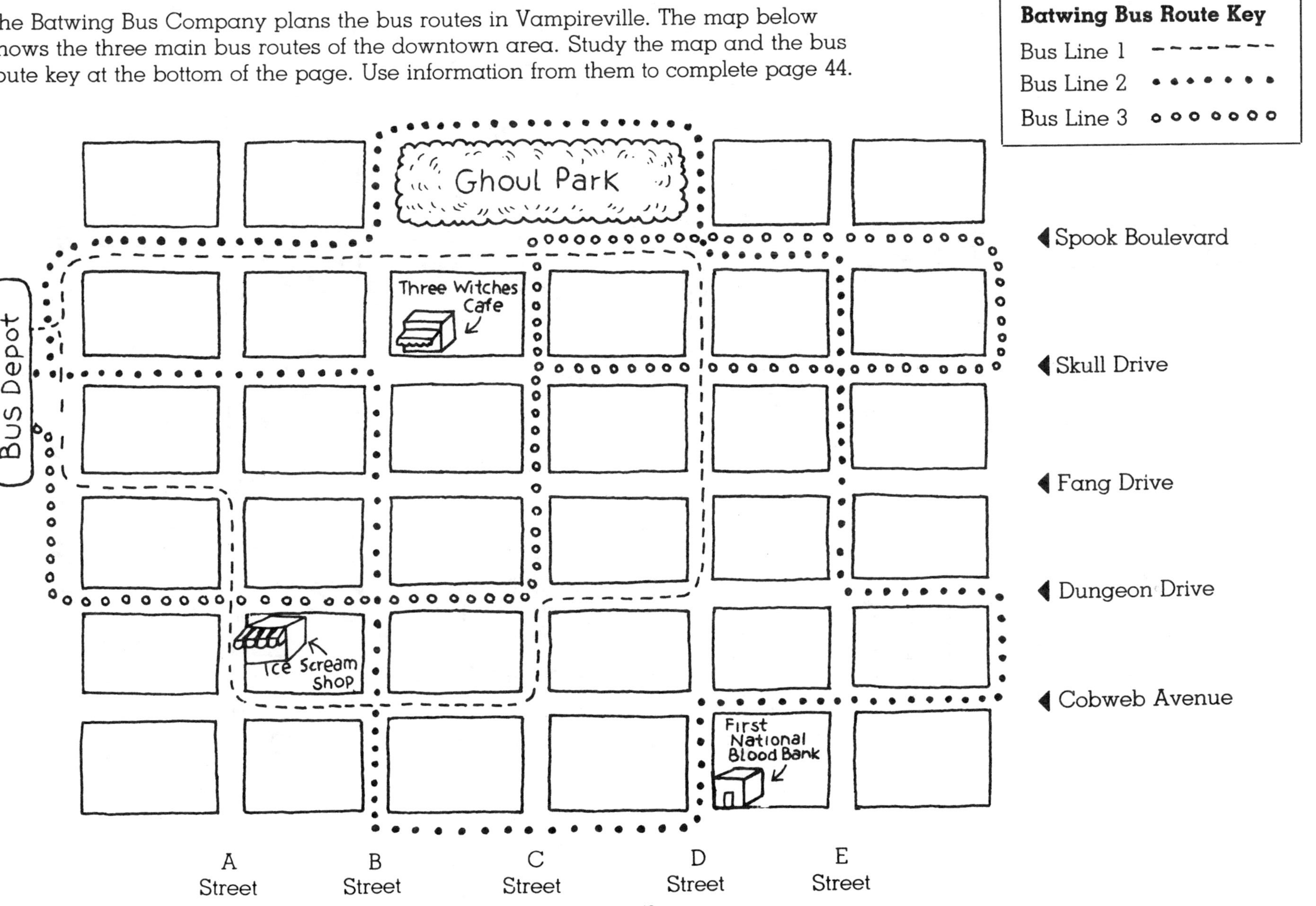

Name ______________________

VISITING VAMPIREVILLE

Use information from the Batwing Bus Company's route map and key on page 43 to answer the questions below. Write your answers on the lines provided.

1. Wilhelmina Witch lives at B Street and Fang Drive. She wants to visit the first National Blood Bank. Which bus line should she take? ______

2. Captain Ghostly's home is on the corner of D Street and Spook Boulevard. All the bus routes pass that corner, but which line has the most direct route to the Ice Scream Shop? ______

3. To go from Dungeon Drive and E Street to Fang Drive and C Street, it's necessary to transfer from one bus to another. Which line would you take first? ______
Where would you transfer? ______________________
To which line would you transfer? ______

4. If you wanted to take an out-of-town visitor for a long ride around Ghoul Park, which bus line would you pick? ______

5. Bert Belfry claims that while he was riding on Bus Line 3 he saw a villainous vampire steal an apple from a stand on the corner of Dungeon Drive and E Street. Was Bert telling the truth? ______
How do you know? ______________________
____

Name ______________________

SWEET SWEETSYLVANIA

Road maps help drivers use roads and highways. The map below shows the main roads and highways in the make-believe state of Sweetsylvania. Look it over. Study the legend. Use this information to answer the questions at the bottom of the page. Write your answers on the lines provided.

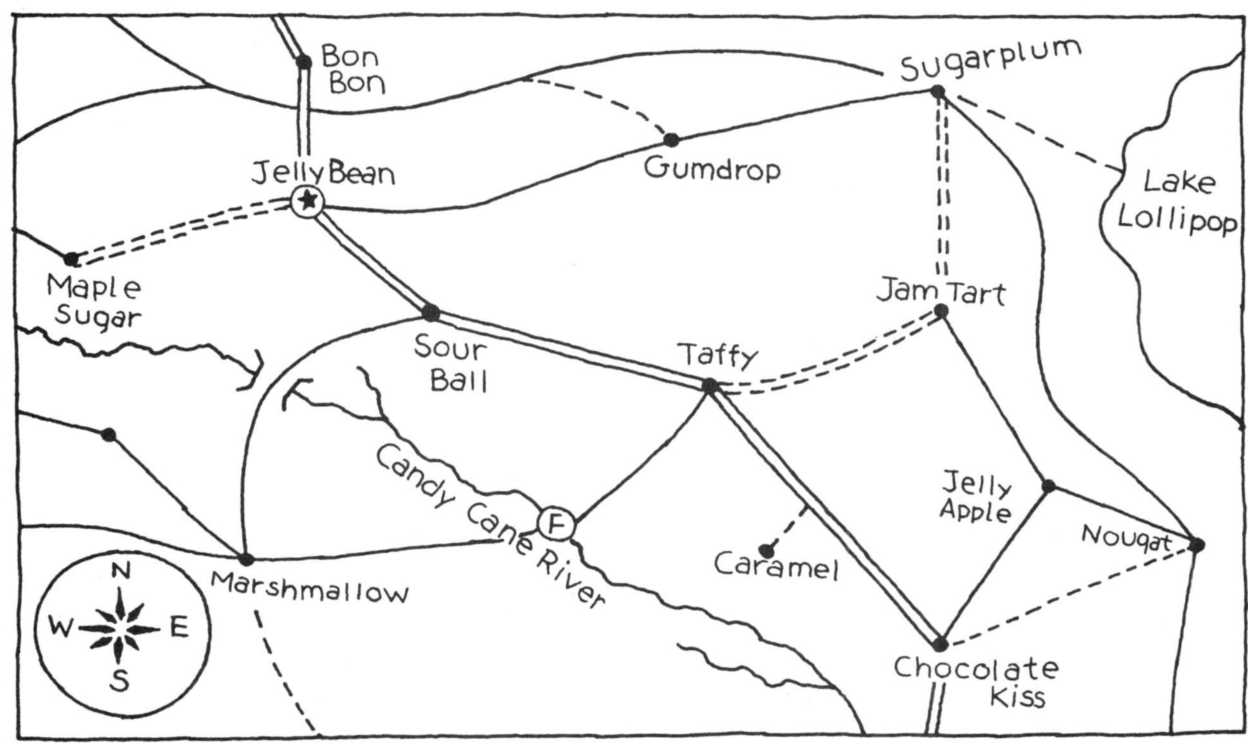

Legend

- ═ highway
- ⁚⁚⁚⁚ highway under construction
- —— two-lane road
- - - - - narrow dirt road
- Ⓕ ferry crossing
-)(bridge

1. What kind of road connects Taffy and Sour Ball? ______________________
2. What kind of road connects Nougat and Jelly Apple? ______________________
3. Why isn't it possible to drive straight through from Jelly Bean to Maple Sugar? ______________________
4. Driving directly from Taffy to Marshmallow, how will you cross the Candy Cane River? ______________________
5. Describe another possible route from Taffy to Marshmallow. ______________________

____

____

Answer Sheet for *Diagrams, Graphs, and Make-Believe Maps*—Section 2

Who's New at the Zoo?—page 28

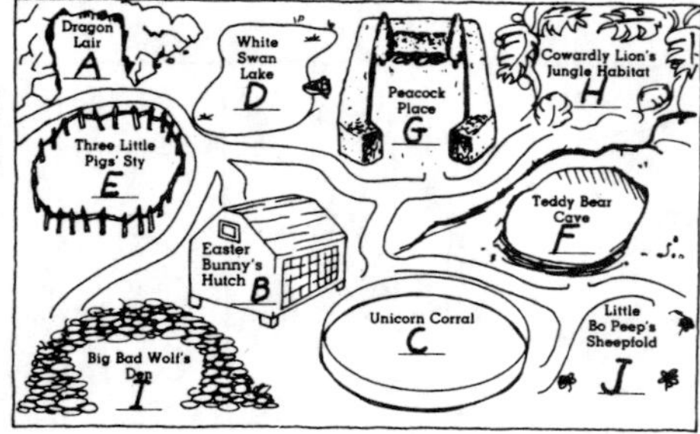

Fantasy Islands—page 29

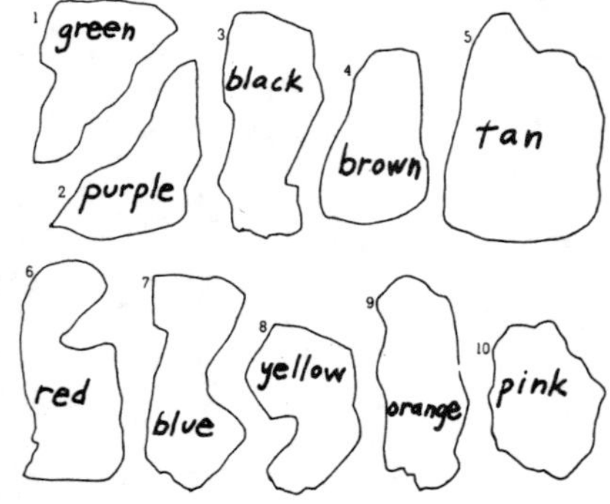

Claude Canary's Escape—page 30

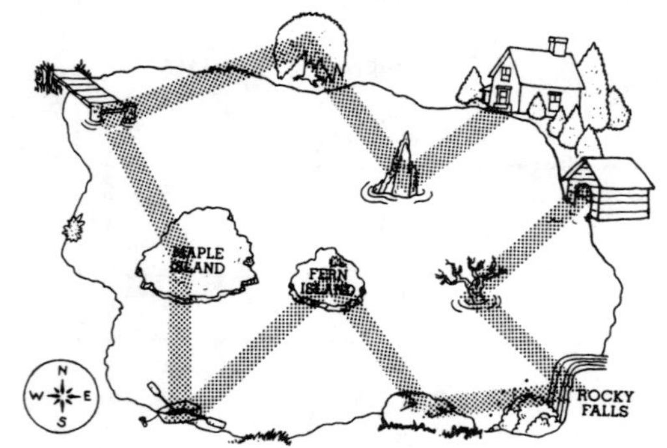

Touchdown Time!—page 31

1. T
2. F
3. F
4. F
5. T

Deliver the Mail—page 32

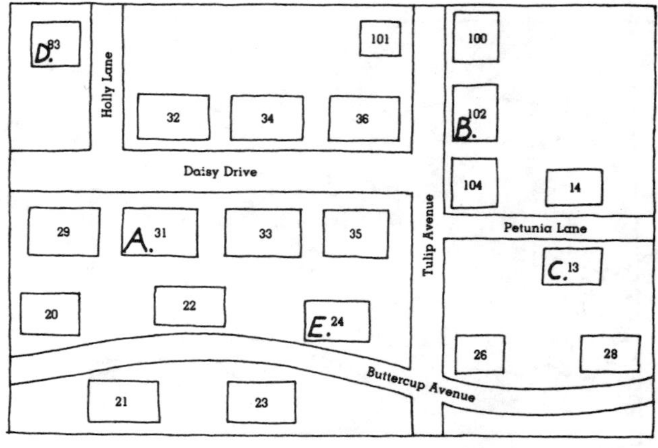

Biking to Henry's House—page 33

1. Loon Lane
2. Berry Avenue
3. left
4. by bridge
5. right
6. right
7. to go around marsh
8. left
9. Rumpus Road
10. Sugar Street

Please Be Seated!—page 34

1. A4; A5
2. F8
3. ▒ and 4. ■

M	109	107	105	103	101	1	2	3	4	5	6	7	8	102	104	106	108	110	M
L	109	107	105	103	101	1	2	3	4	5	6	7	8	102	104	106	108	110	L
K	109	107	105	103	101	1	2	spotlights and video camera			6	7	8	102	104	106	108	110	K
J	109	107	105	103	101	1	2	3	4	5	6	7	8	102	104	106	108	110	J
H	109	107	105	103	101	1	2	3	4	5	6	7	8	102	104	106	108	110	H
G	109	107	105	103	101	1	2	3	4	5	6	7	8	102	104	106	108	110	G
F	109	107	105	103	101	1	2	3	4	5	6	7	8	102	104	106	108	110	F
E	109	107	105	103	101	1	2	3	4	5	6	7	8	102	104	106	108	110	E
D	109	107	105	103	101	1	2	3	4	5	6	7	8					110	D
C	109	107	105	103	101	1	2	3	4	5	6	7	8	102	104	106	108	110	C
B	109	107	105	103	101	1	2	3	4	5	6	7	8	102	104	106	108	110	B
A	109	107	105	103	101	1	2	3	4	5	6	7	8	102	104	106	108	110	A

5. He is seated behind the spotlights and video camera and can't see very well.

Swing Around the Sun—page 35

1. Mercury
2. Pluto
3. Saturn
4. Venus; Mars
5. Mars; Jupiter

Answer Sheet for *Diagrams, Graphs, and Make-Believe Maps*—Section 2

Playground Plan—page 36

Answers will vary.

View from the Top—page 37

Oh No, More Snow!—page 38

1. January
2. 21
3. 3; 6; 1
4. July; August
5. March; 3

Dollars and Cakes—page 39

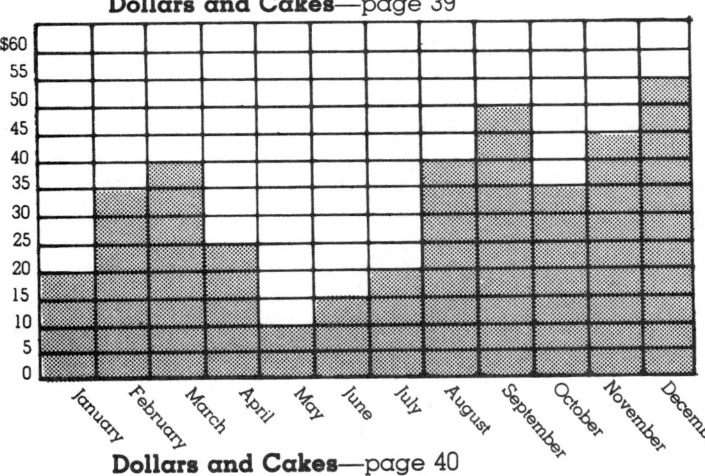

Dollars and Cakes—page 40

1. a. December
   b. $55
2. a. May
   b. $10
3. a. July to December
   b. $245
4. a. $15
   b. $10
5. a. $390
   b. $32.50

On the Road Again—page 42

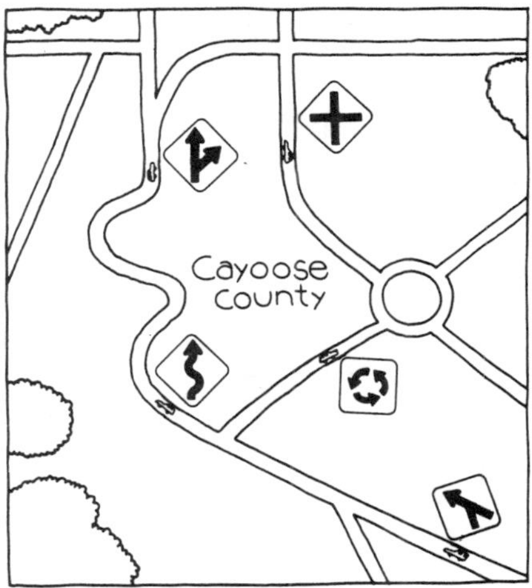

Visiting Vampireville—page 44

1. 2
2. 3
3. 2; E Street and Skull Drive; 3
4. 2
5. No; Bus Line 3 doesn't pass the corner of Dungeon Drive and E Street.

Sweet Sweetsylvania—page 45

1. highway
2. two-lane road
3. The highway is under construction.
4. by ferry
5. Go from Taffy to Sour Ball and then to Marshmallow.

Name ______________________

FIND THE HIDDEN STATE

Look at the puzzle below. A mystery state is hiding inside it. To find it, use a pencil to fill in all the spaces marked with an **X**. Do not fill in the spaces marked with an **O**.

After you have completed the puzzle, answer the questions at the bottom of the page. Write your answers on the lines provided. (Use a map or an atlas to help you.)

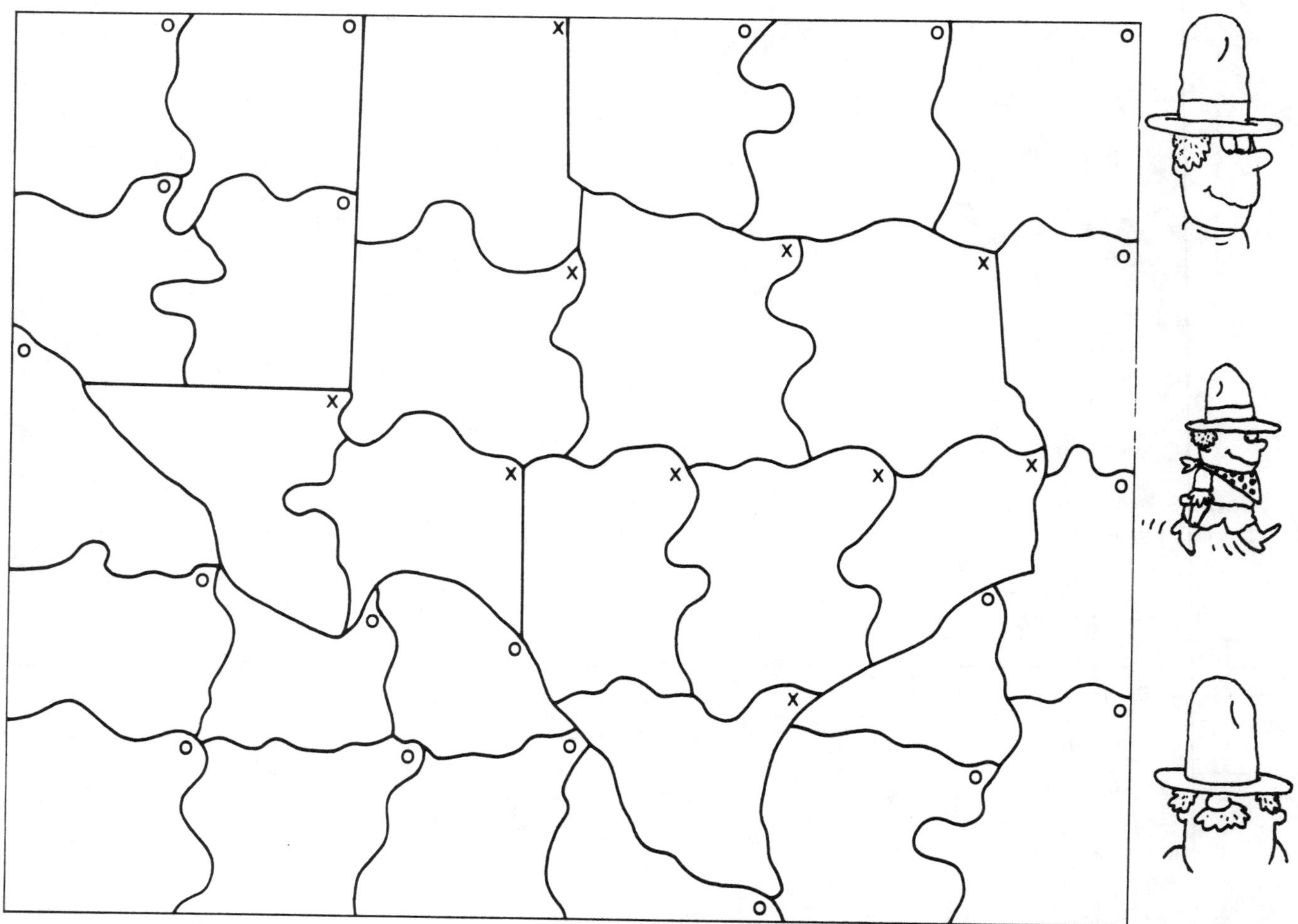

1. The name of this state is ______________________.
2. The capital of this state is ______________________.
3. This state is bounded by four other states. Name them.

   ______________________.
4. On its southeastern edge, this state is bounded by a large body of water called the

   ______________________.
5. This state also shares a long river border with a neighboring country.

   The country is ______________________.

Name ______________________________

CALIFORNIA CRISIS

Cousin Madeline Mapmaker, who prints beautifully, often prints the words on the Mapmaker family's maps. Today she is supposed to finish a map of California. Unfortunately, she has just polished her nails, and the polish isn't dry yet.

You can help Cousin Madeline. Look at the map of California below. Then read the instructions on page 50 to complete it.

Name ______________________

CALIFORNIA CRISIS

Read the instructions below. Then, with the help of a printed map of California and its neighbors, write in the names of places on the map on page 49 as instructed. Write the names on the lines provided.

1. On the map, write the name of the ocean that borders California on the west.
2. What country borders California on the south? Write its name on the map.
3. What state borders California on the north? Write its name on the map.
4. Find the capital city symbol on the map. Write the name of California's capital in the correct place.
5. Northeast of the city of Fresno is a famous national park. Write the name of the park on the map.
6. Two other national parks are east of Fresno. One is Sequoia National Park. Write the name of the other one on the map.
7. To the southeast of Bakersfield is a large desert area. Write the name of the desert on the map.
8. On the California coast, not far from the southern border, is a large port city. Write the name of this city in the correct place on the map.
9. A river forms part of California's southeast boundary. Write the name of this river on the map.
10. There are a number of islands off the coast of southern California. One of these is missing its name. Write it in.

Name ______________________________

RHODE ISLAND ROAD TRIP

Some members of the Happy Wanderers are planning a bicycle tour of Rhode Island, the smallest state in the United States. Una Cycle is in charge of finding information about the state for the other members of the travelers' club. You can help her. Look at the map of Rhode Island below. Notice the compass rose, the map legend, and the mileage scale. Use this information to answer the questions at the bottom of the page. Write your answers on the lines provided. (You will need a ruler to answer question 4.)

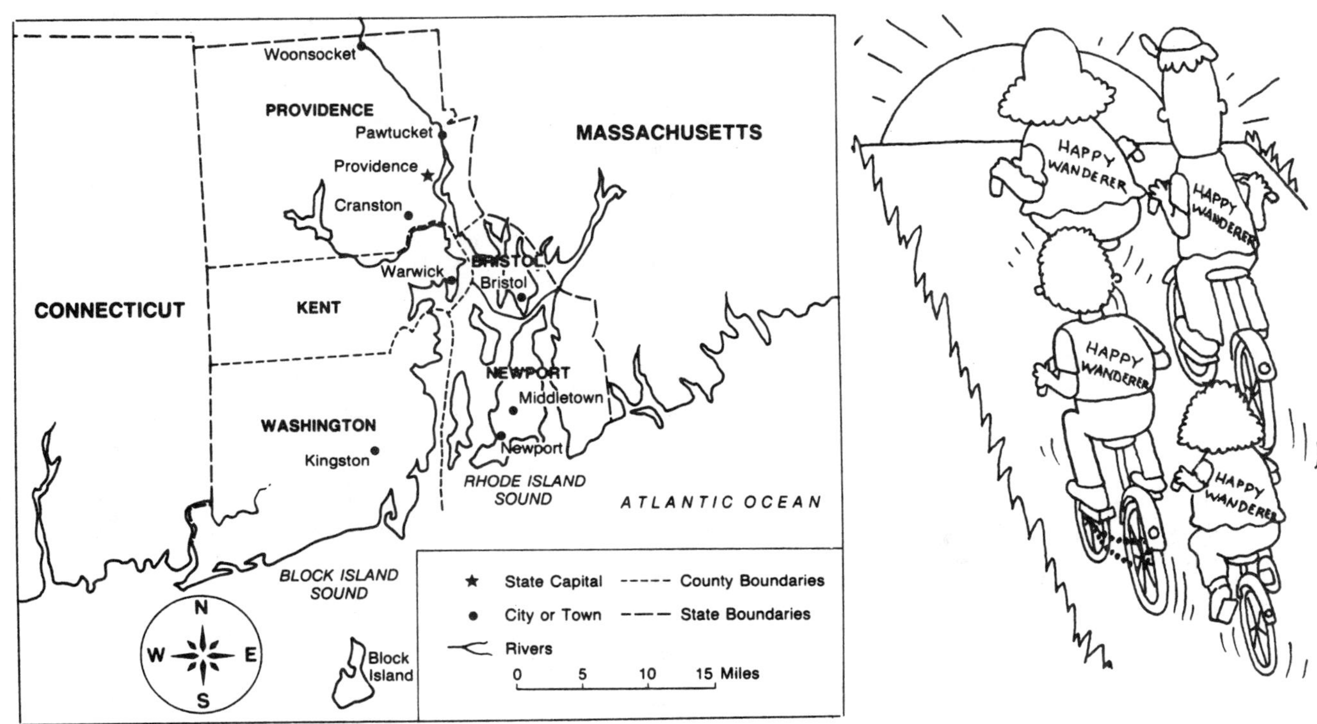

1. The trip will begin in Woonsocket. From there they will pedal to Pawtucket. In which direction will they travel, south, southwest, or southeast?

   ____

2. From Pawtucket, the group will continue on to the state capital. What is its name? ______________________________
3. From the state capital, the bikers will ride to Warwick. What county is Warwick in? ______________________________
4. After eating lunch in Warwick, the bikers will continue on to Kingston. They don't want to ride more than 25 to 30 miles in the afternoon. According to the map, do they seem to have enough time to reach Kingston by suppertime? ______________
5. Kingston is about how many miles from Newport—5, 10, or 15? ______________

   Can the bikers cover this distance on their bikes? Why or why not? ______________

   ____

Name ______________________________

BOSTON BRANCH

The Happy Wanderers are opening a branch office in Boston. Otto Mobile will be in charge of the operation. He has decided to live in a nearby town and commute to work by car. To help him decide which town he would like to live in, he has been studying a road map of Boston and its surrounding towns.

Help Otto make his choice. Look carefully at the map below. Study the compass rose, the map legend, and the scale of miles. Use this information to answer the questions at the bottom of the page. Write your answers on the lines provided.

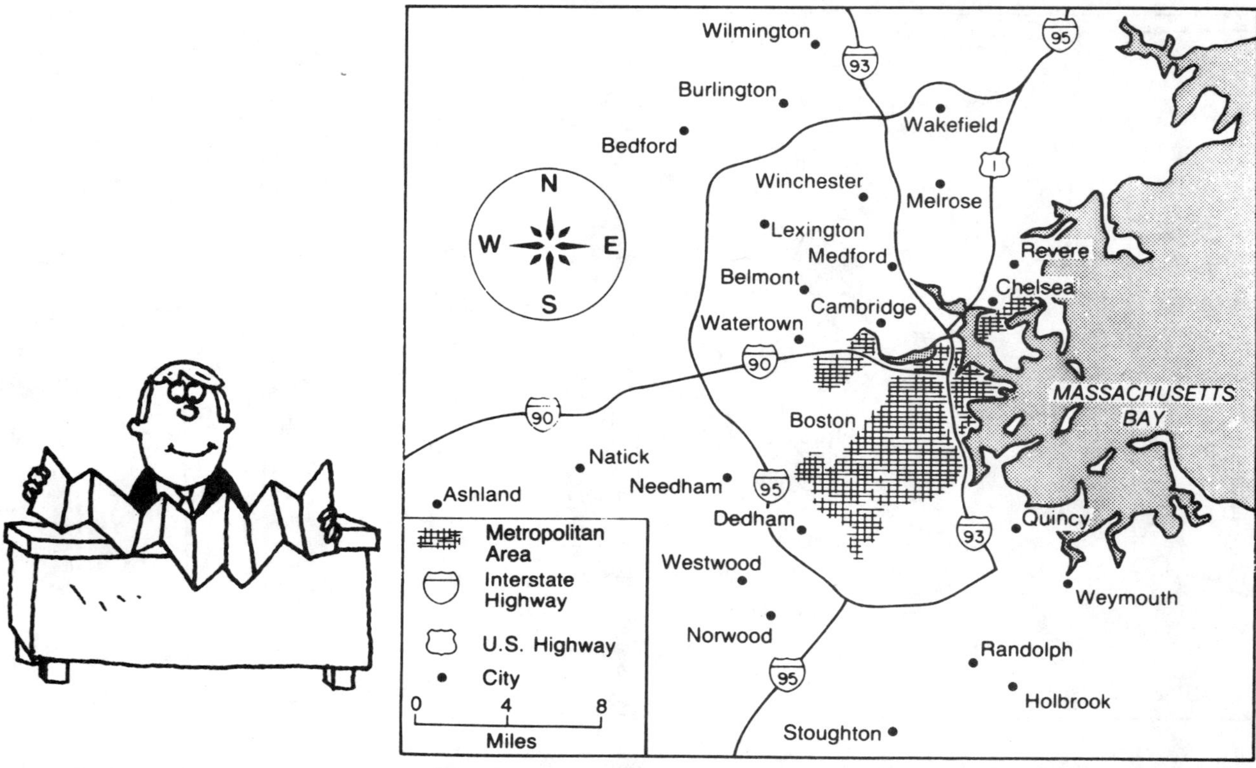

1. If Otto rents a house in Medford, on which interstate highway could he drive to work? ______________________________

2. If Otto decides to live in Ashland, about how many miles would he be from the nearest highway—2, 5, or 12? ______________________________

3. Otto notices that one interstate highway makes a half-circle around Boston on the west. What is its number? ______________________________
Which three of the following towns—Wakefield, Burlington, Revere, Weymouth, Dedham, and Cambridge—lie closest to this highway? ______________________________
____

4. Otto may rent an apartment in Melrose. From there he can take either of two highways to reach Boston. What are their numbers?

   Interstate Highway ______________________________

   U.S. Highway ______________________________

Name ____________________

NOTE ON THE NEWEST STATES

When Margaret Mabel Mapmaker came home from school today, she found two unfinished maps and this note:

> Dear Margaret Mabel,
> I had to rush off to the supermarket and didn't have time to finish these maps. Please finish them for me. First label each state correctly. One is Alaska. The other is Hawaii. Then write the names of their capital cities. We also need to show a major product for each state. Draw the symbol for oil for the Alaska map. Make up a symbol for pineapples and draw it for the Hawaii map. Use the symbol chart and an atlas to help you. Write only on the lines and draw only in the boxes.
> Thanks a heap, dear. Be back soon.
>
> Love,
> Mom

Margaret Mabel would like to help her mom, but she has a lot of homework to do. You can do the job for her. Just follow the instructions in the letter.

State: ____________________

Capital City: ____________________

A Major Product:

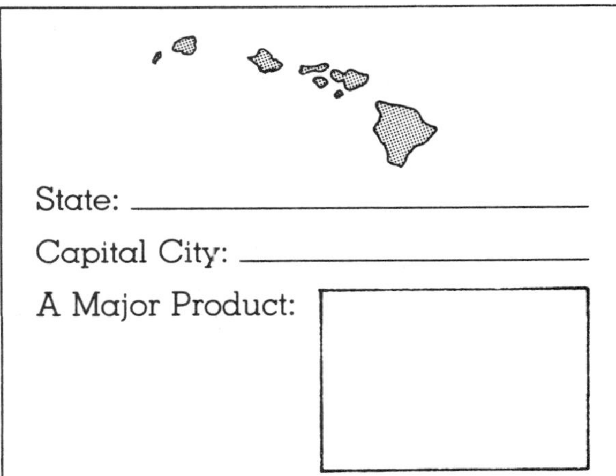

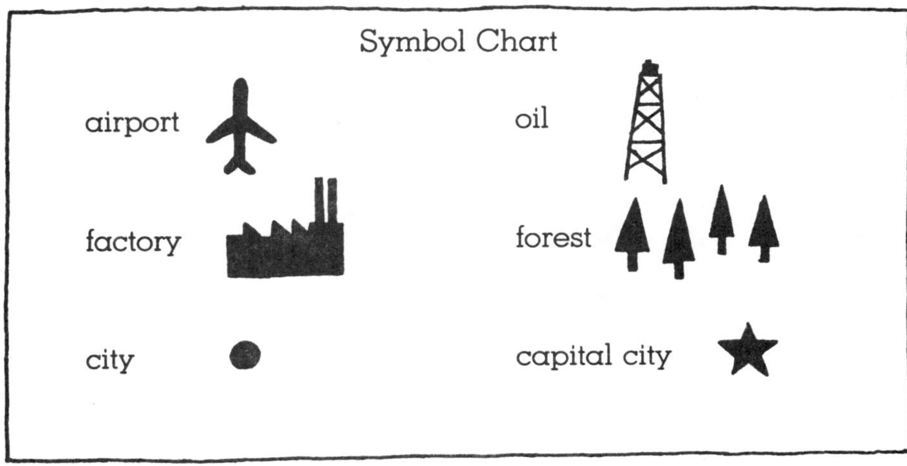

Name ______________________

STATES OF CONFUSION

Two members of the Happy Wanderers, Walker Foote and Mary Shanks, want to hike through every state that was once part of the original 13 colonies. They have a list of these states and they have a map of the eastern seaboard of the United States where these states are located. But the map is missing the states' names so they don't know which state is which!

Help Walker and Mary end their confusion. Look at the map below. Read the list of state names. On the line next to each name, write the letter of the correct state. Use an atlas to help you. Three have been done for you.

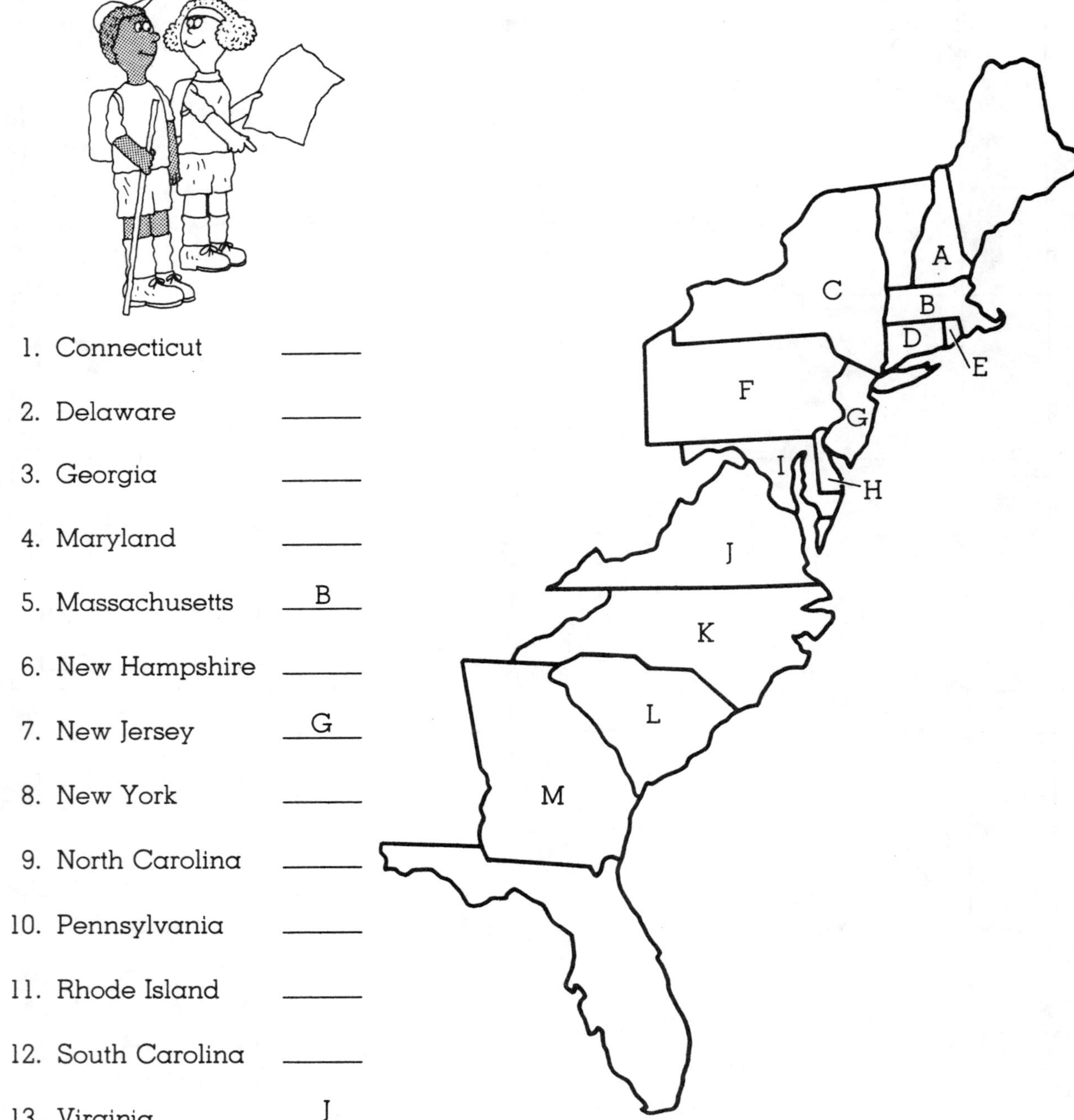

1. Connecticut ______
2. Delaware ______
3. Georgia ______
4. Maryland ______
5. Massachusetts __B__
6. New Hampshire ______
7. New Jersey __G__
8. New York ______
9. North Carolina ______
10. Pennsylvania ______
11. Rhode Island ______
12. South Carolina ______
13. Virginia __J__

Name ______________________

PUZZLING STATES

For her birthday, Margaret Mabel Mapmaker received a jigsaw puzzle of the United States. Each piece is in the shape of a state. Unfortunately, her brother Little Map has scratched off the state names and capital cities from 10 of the puzzle pieces. Margaret Mabel knows the names of the 10 states missing from her puzzle, but she doesn't know which name goes with which state.

Before she gets any angrier with her little brother, help Margaret Mabel solve her problem. Look at the state shapes below. Read the list of names. Use a map of the United States to identify each shape. Write the letter of each state shape on the line next to the correct name. Then, on the line under the name of each state, write the name of its capital city.

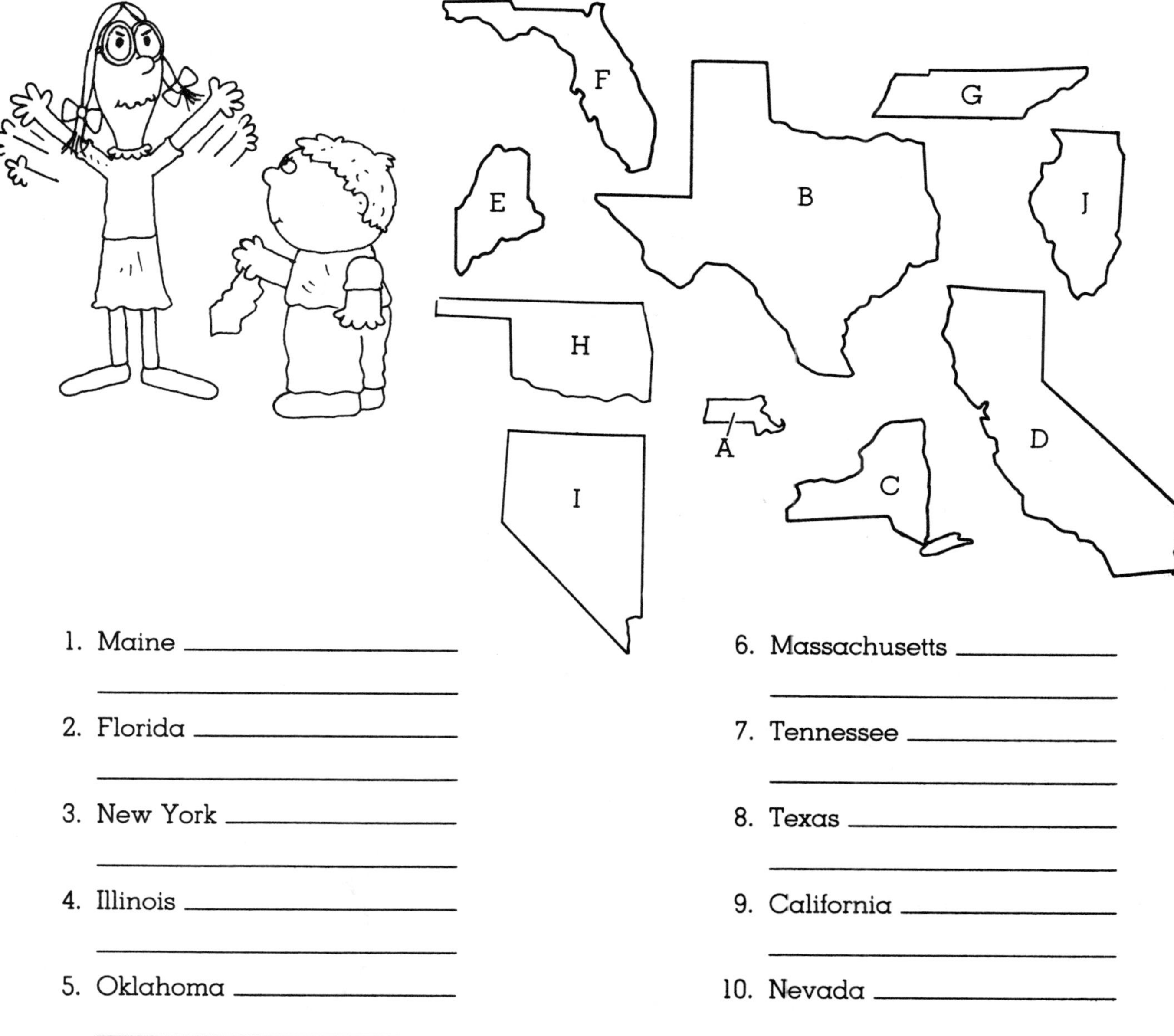

1. Maine ______________________
   ____
2. Florida ______________________
   ____
3. New York ______________________
   ____
4. Illinois ______________________
   ____
5. Oklahoma ______________________
   ____
6. Massachusetts ______________________
   ____
7. Tennessee ______________________
   ____
8. Texas ______________________
   ____
9. California ______________________
   ____
10. Nevada ______________________
    ____

Name ____________________

CORNY'S NEBRASKA CORNBREAD

Cornelius "Corny" Husks is the new sales manager for the Nebraska Cornbread Bakery. It's his job to plan the delivery routes for the bakery's trucks. You can help. Look at the Nebraska state map below. Use it to help you follow the instructions on page 57.

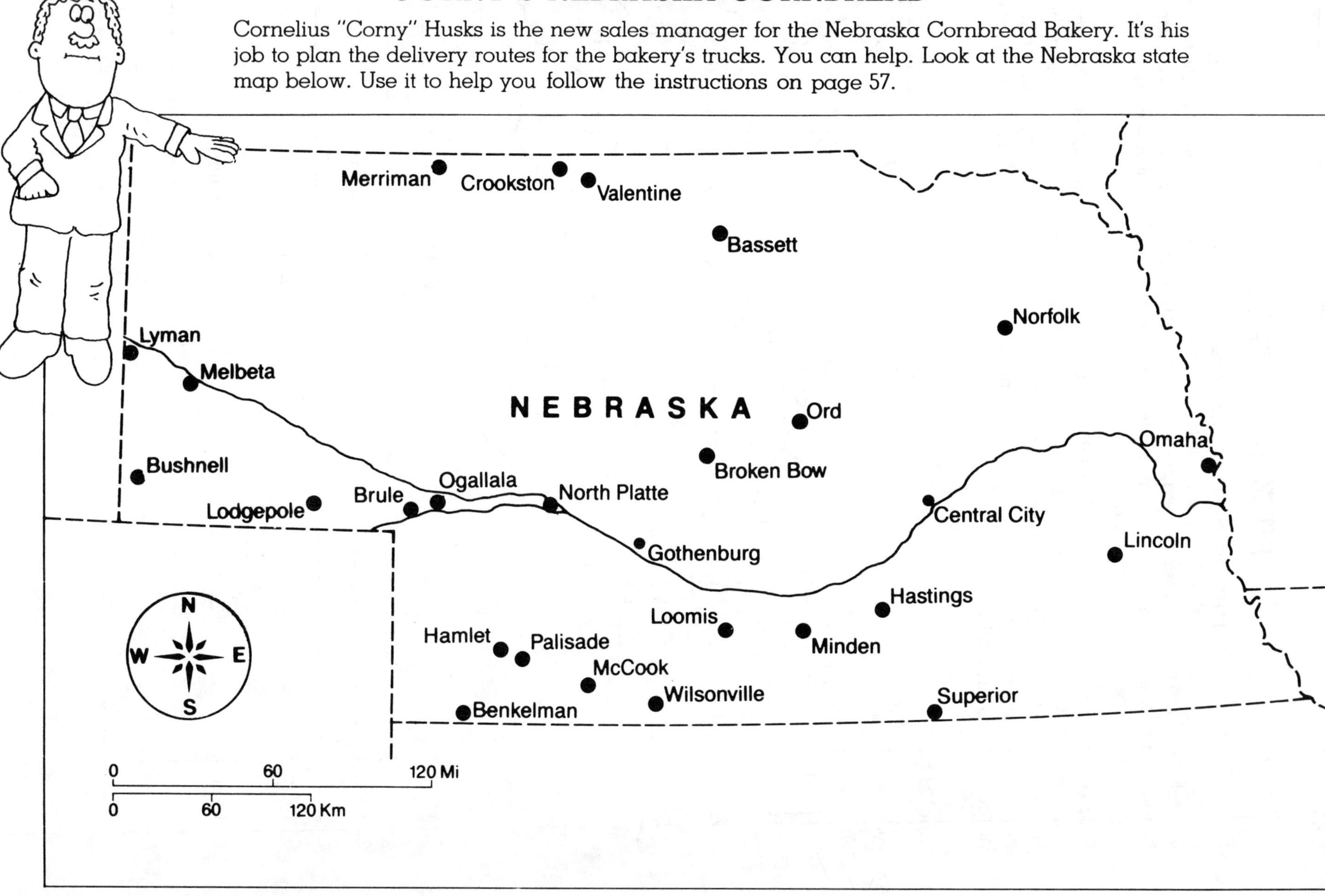

Name ___________________________

CORNY'S NEBRASKA CORNBREAD

As sales manager of the Nebraska Cornbread Bakery, Corny has to plan the delivery routes. Read the instructions below. Then use colored pencils and the map on page 56 to help Corny draw his routes.

1. The Nebraska Cornbread Bakery has five supply warehouses in the state of Nebraska. They are in Omaha, Bassett, North Platte, McCook, and Lincoln. Locate these places on the map. Print a W (for warehouse) next to each one.

2. Each warehouse delivers to a network of local towns. The chart below shows each supply network. Use this information to draw each route on the map on page 56 by placing **an X** on the towns for each network. Then connect each point. Use a different colored pencil for each network.

Warehouse location	**Omaha**	**Bassett**	**North Platte**	**McCook**	**Lincoln**
Delivers to:	Norfolk Ord Broken Bow Gothenburg Central City	Valentine Crookston Merriman	Ogallala Brule Lodgepole Bushnell Melbeta Lyman	Palisade Hamlet Benkelman Wilsonville Loomis	Superior Minden Hastings

Name ____________________

ROADS FOR PUERTO RICO

Uncle Mac Mapmaker is learning how to draw roads on maps. His assignment for tonight is to draw some imaginary roads on a map of Puerto Rico. Unfortunately, he has fallen asleep over his homework.

See if you can complete Uncle Mac's assignment. Look at the map below. Notice the road symbols. Then follow the instructions at the bottom of the page to draw an imaginary road network for Puerto Rico.

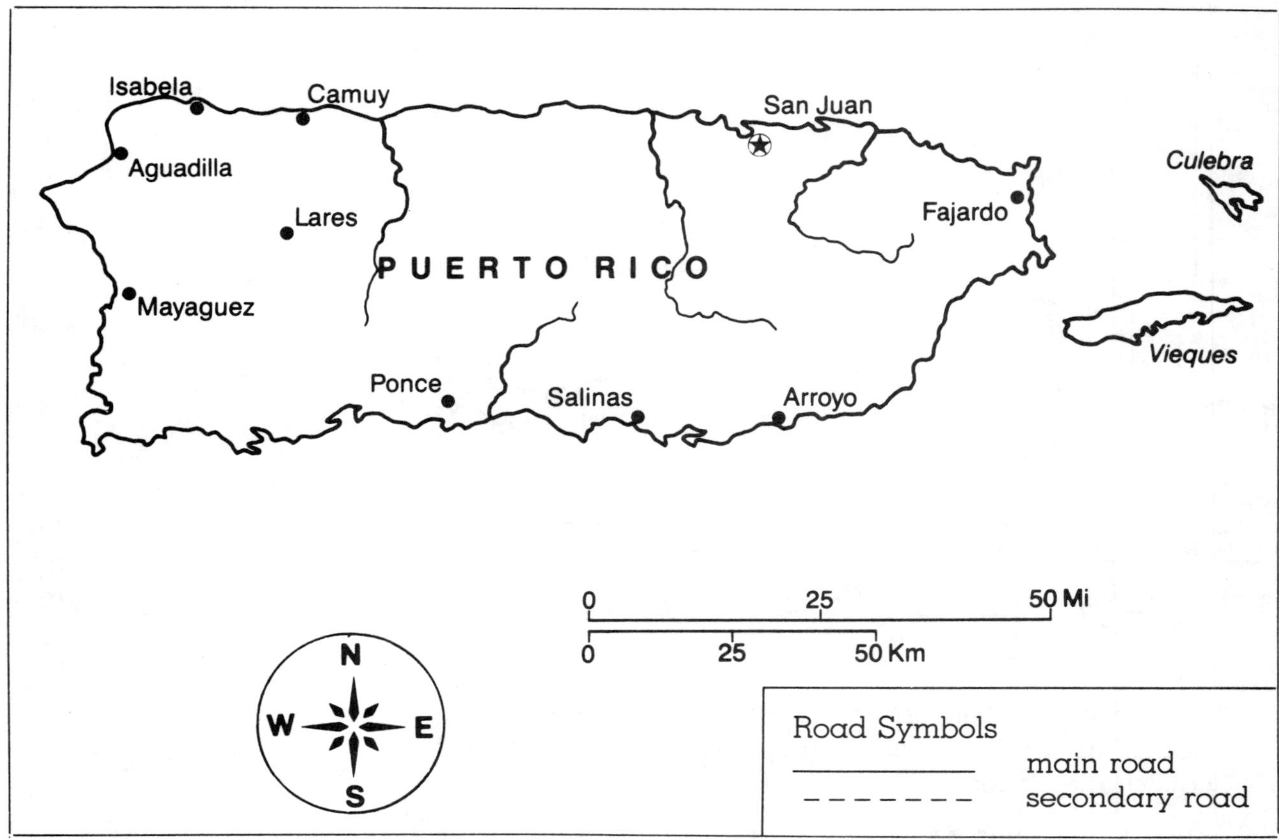

1. Using a blue pencil and the correct symbol, draw a main road around the perimeter of the island, as follows:
   San Juan to Fajardo, from Fajardo to Arroyo, and from there to Salinas and Ponce. From Ponce, continue northwest to Mayaguez and then north to Aguadilla. From Aguadilla, continue northeast to Isabela, then east to Camuy and San Juan.
2. Using a red pencil and the correct symbol, draw your secondary roads as follows:
   a. Isabela to Lares to Ponce.

   b. Mayaguez to Lares.
   c. Aguadilla to Camuy to Lares.
   d. San Juan to Arroyo.
   e. Lares to Salinas to Fajardo.

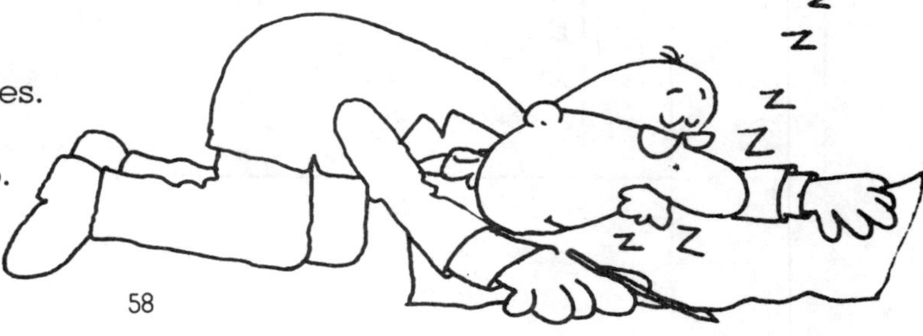

Name ______________________________

QUEBEC QUESTIONS

Jane Plane—business person, amateur pilot, and member of the Happy Wanderers—is planning a flying tour of the Canadian province of Quebec. Jane wants to know about Quebec's industries. She has made up a list of questions that she would like answered before she begins her trip. To find the answers, she is looking at the industry map of Quebec, below.

Read Jane's questions. Then study the map. Using this information, see if you can find the answers to Jane's questions. Write your answers on the lines provided.

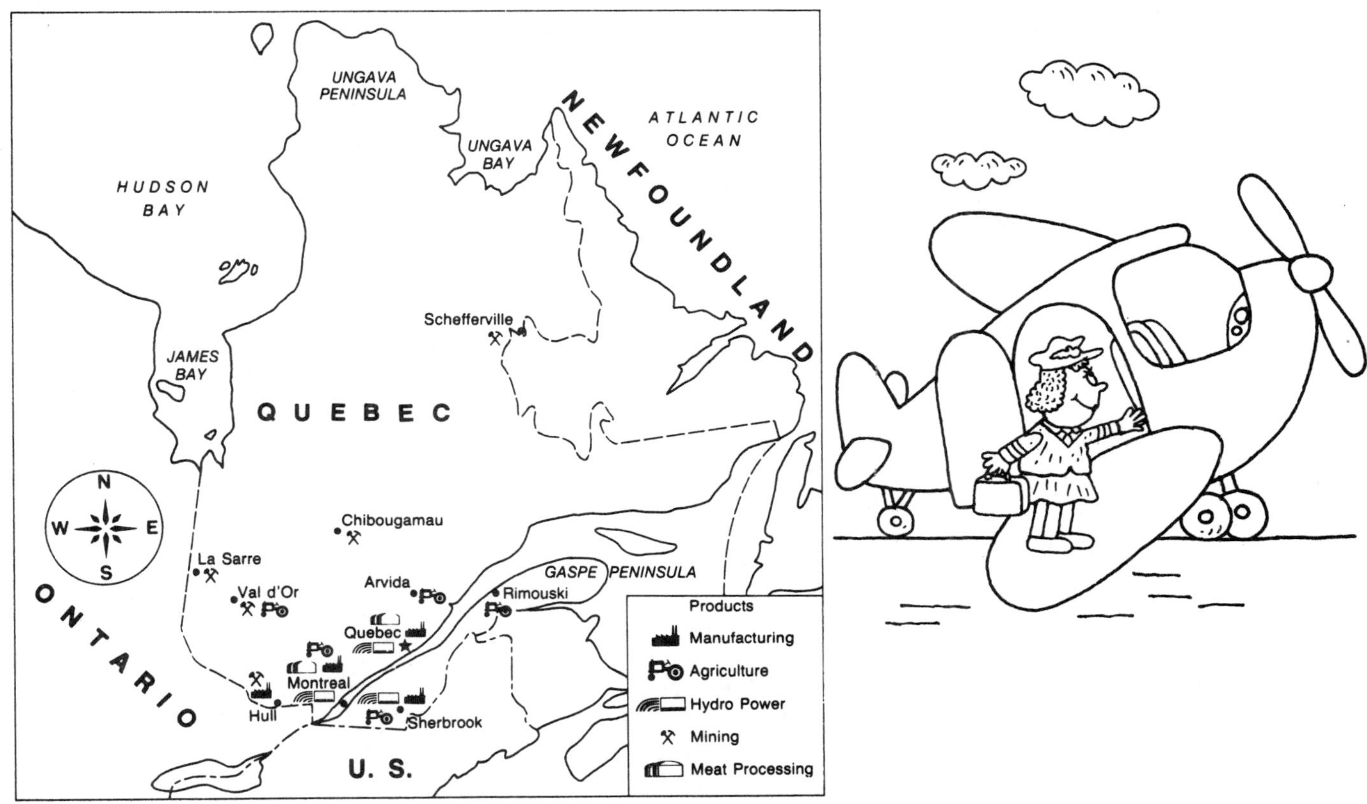

1. Which five Quebec cities are mining centers? ______________________________

____

2. In which part of the province is manufacturing concentrated–the east, west, north, or south? ______________________________

____

3. Where could one expect to find the greatest number of farmers, near Schefferville, Rimouski, or the city of Quebec? ______________________________

____

4. Of these three industries—manufacturing, hydropower, and meat processing—which is not shown near Sherbrook? ______________________________

____

Name ______________________________

CAPE COD CRUISE

Five members of the Happy Wanderers—Dory Dinghy, Skip Skiff, Sam Pan, Win Jammer, and Tug Boat—love to go on sailing cruises with Captain Sloop Schooner on his ship, *Out to Launch*. On their last cruise—around Cape Cod, off the coast of Massachusetts—they had a more exciting time than they bargained for!

Read the incidents in the ship's log below. Then use this information to complete pages 61 and 62.

Friday, July 22. Today we set sail from Edgartown on Martha's Vineyard and sailed northeast through Nantucket Sound. At 41° 30′N lat., 70° 10′W long. we realized we'd forgotten to buy food for the trip. We turned and sailed southeast to the town of Nantucket on the island of Nantucket to stock up.

Saturday, July 23. Today we set sail from Nantucket and, narrowly skirting the tip of the island, sailed northeast into the Atlantic Ocean. Curving around the east coast of Cape Cod, we continued northwest to 42° 10′N lat., 70° 10′W long. There we lay at anchor for a few hours. Tug, who had been showing off by climbing the mast, fell overboard and had to be rescued. We spent the night at sea.

Sunday, July 24. Today we intended to sail around the tip of Cape Cod, but a storm suddenly arose and blew us off course. We reached 42° 0′N lat., 70° 30′W long. before the storm died down. Then there was no wind at all and we couldn't move.

Monday, July 25. We are still here.

Tuesday, July 26. Still here.

Wednesday, July 27. Ditto.

Thursday, July 28. A wind finally sprang up and we set sail. Unfortunately, in our excitement, we didn't pay attention to where we were going. We sailed to 41° 50′N lat., 70° 10′W long. before we realized we were off course. Turning around, we sailed due north and, thirsty, sore, sunburned, and tired, finally arrived in Provincetown.

Name ______________________

CAPE COD CRUISE

Read the incidents in the ship's log on page 60. Read about latitude and longitude as explained below. Then read the information below about locating a point on this map as you look at the map on page 62. (For a more detailed introduction, read pages 19 and 20.) Use this information to draw a line on the map showing the course taken by the *Out to Launch* on its cruise.

How to Find Latitude and Longitude

Lines of latitude (lat.) and longitude (long.) are imaginary lines drawn on maps to help us locate places. Lines of latitude run sideways, circling the globe east and west. Lines of longitude run up and down, circling the globe north and south.

Both kinds of lines are measured in degrees (°). On maps that show small areas, the degrees are divided into *minutes* (′). There are 60 minutes between every degree of latitude and longitude.

How to locate a point on this map

1. Find the correct line of latitude:
   a. Look in the right- or left-hand margin for the degree number. (41° is on the bottom line.)
   b. Move one finger up the column of numbers until you find the minute number. Keep it there. (20′ is two lines up from the bottom.)
2. Find the correct line of longitude:
   a. Look in the top or bottom row of numbers for the degree number. (70° is one line in from the right.)
   b. Use a finger on your other hand to move left along the row of numbers until you find the minute number. (10′ is two lines in from the right.)
3. Move both of your fingers to the point where the lines of latitude and longitude meet.

Name______________________________

CAPE COD CRUISE

Look at the map of Cape Cod below. Use information from pages 60 and 61 to trace the route of the *Out to Launch* on it.

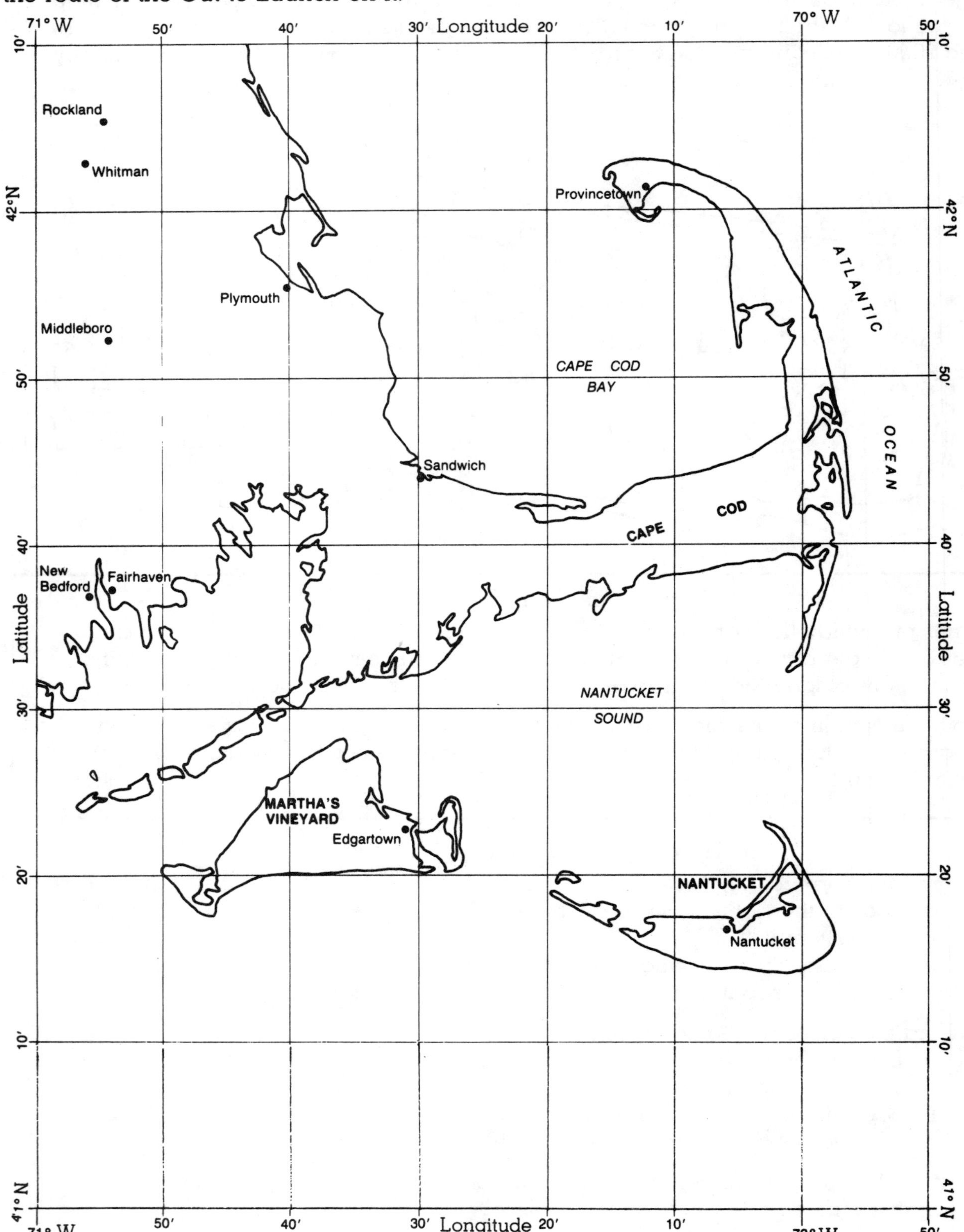

Answer Sheet for *Close to Home*—Section 3

Find the Hidden State—page 48

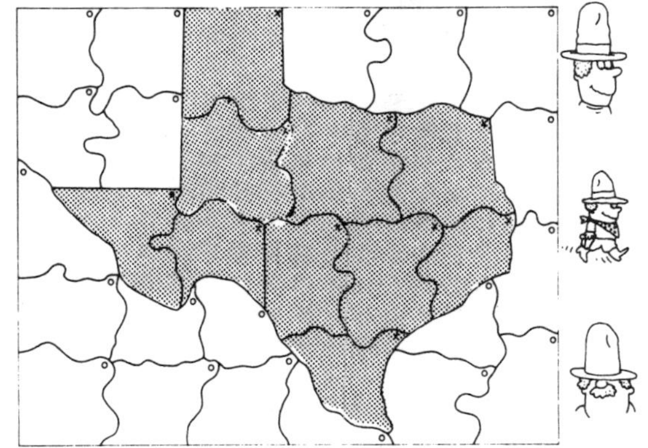

1. Texas
2. Austin
3. New Mexico, Oklahoma, Arkansas, Louisiana
4. Gulf of Mexico
5. Mexico

California Crisis—page 49

Rhode Island Road Trip—page 51

1. southeast
2. Providence
3. Kent
4. Yes.
5. 10; No. Rhode Island Sound is in the way.

Boston Branch—page 52

1. 93
2. 2
3. 95; Wakefield, Burlington, Dedham
4. 93; 1

Note on the Newest States—page 53

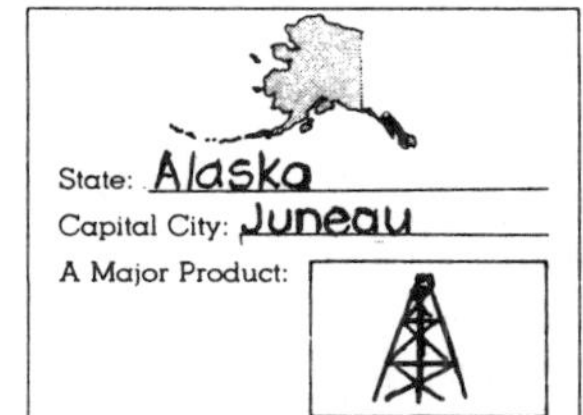

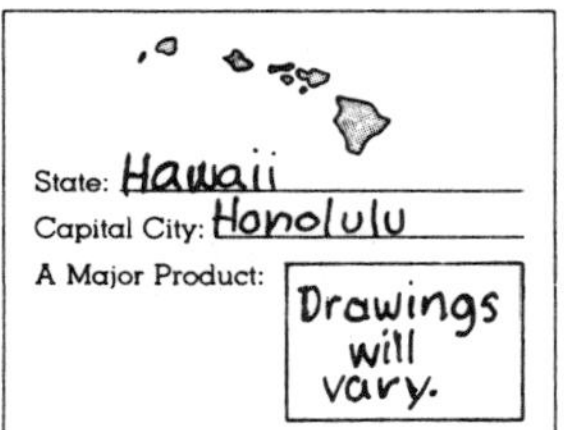

States of Confusion—page 54

1. D
2. H
3. M
4. I
5. (B)
6. A
7. (G)
8. C
9. K
10. F
11. E
12. L
13. (J)

Puzzling States—page 55

1. E; Augusta
2. F; Tallahassee
3. C; Albany
4. J; Springfield
5. H; Oklahoma City
6. A; Boston
7. G; Nashville
8. B; Austin
9. D; Sacramento
10. I; Carson City

Answer Sheet for *Close to Home*—Section 3

Corny's Nebraska Cornbread—page 56

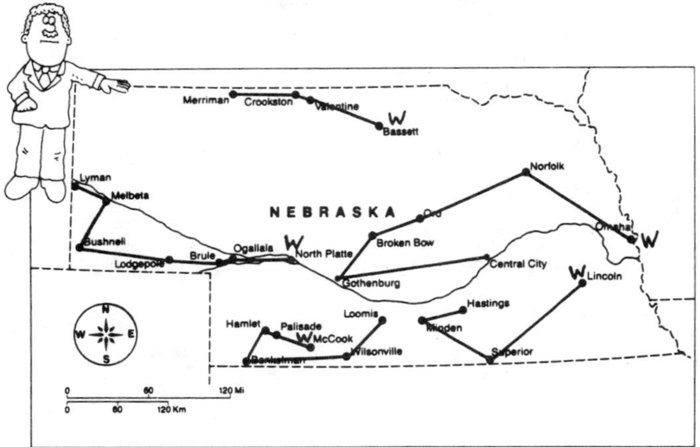

Roads for Puerto Rico—page 58

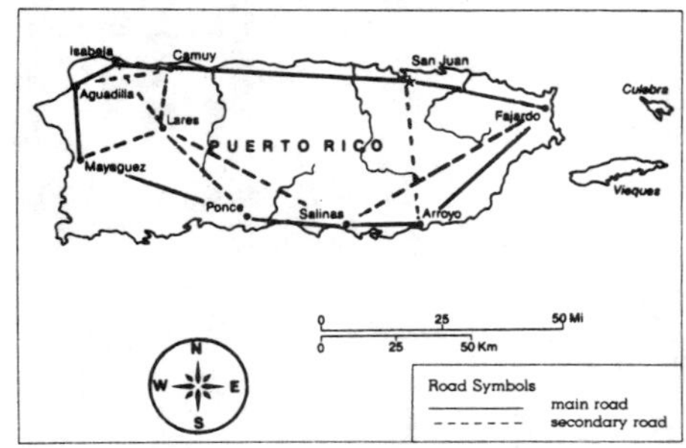

Quebec Questions—page 59

1. Schefferville, Chibougamau, La Sarre, Val d'Or, Hull
2. south
3. Rimouski
4. meat processing

Cape Cod Cruise—page 62

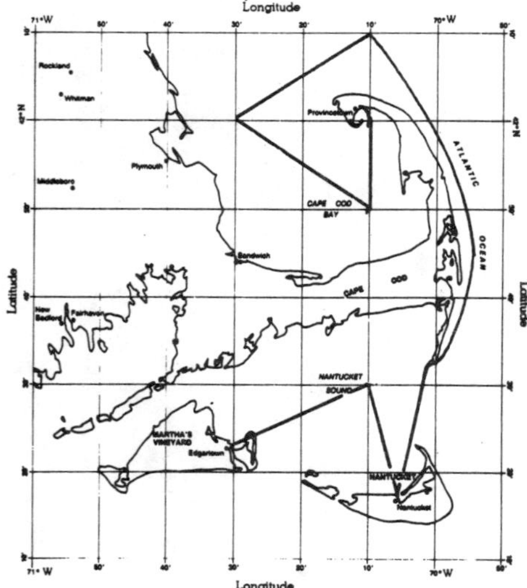

Name ______________________

COLORFUL COUNTRIES

When Maudie Mapmaker finishes drawing a map, she often colors it in. Colors are useful on maps. They can help to show where one country or state ends and another begins. They also help to separate land and water areas.

Look at the map below that Maudie has just drawn. It shows the countries of Canada and the United States and some of their neighbors. Maudie's son, Little Map, would like to color it in. But Maudie won't let him because he always colors everything red and scribbles outside the lines.

Give Maudie a hand. Using crayons or colored pencils, color in each country. Use these colors: red, green, yellow, brown, and orange. You may use the same color for more than one country, but use different colors for countries which are next to each other. (Remember that Alaska and Puerto Rico belong to the United States.) Then color the water areas blue. Use an atlas to help you.

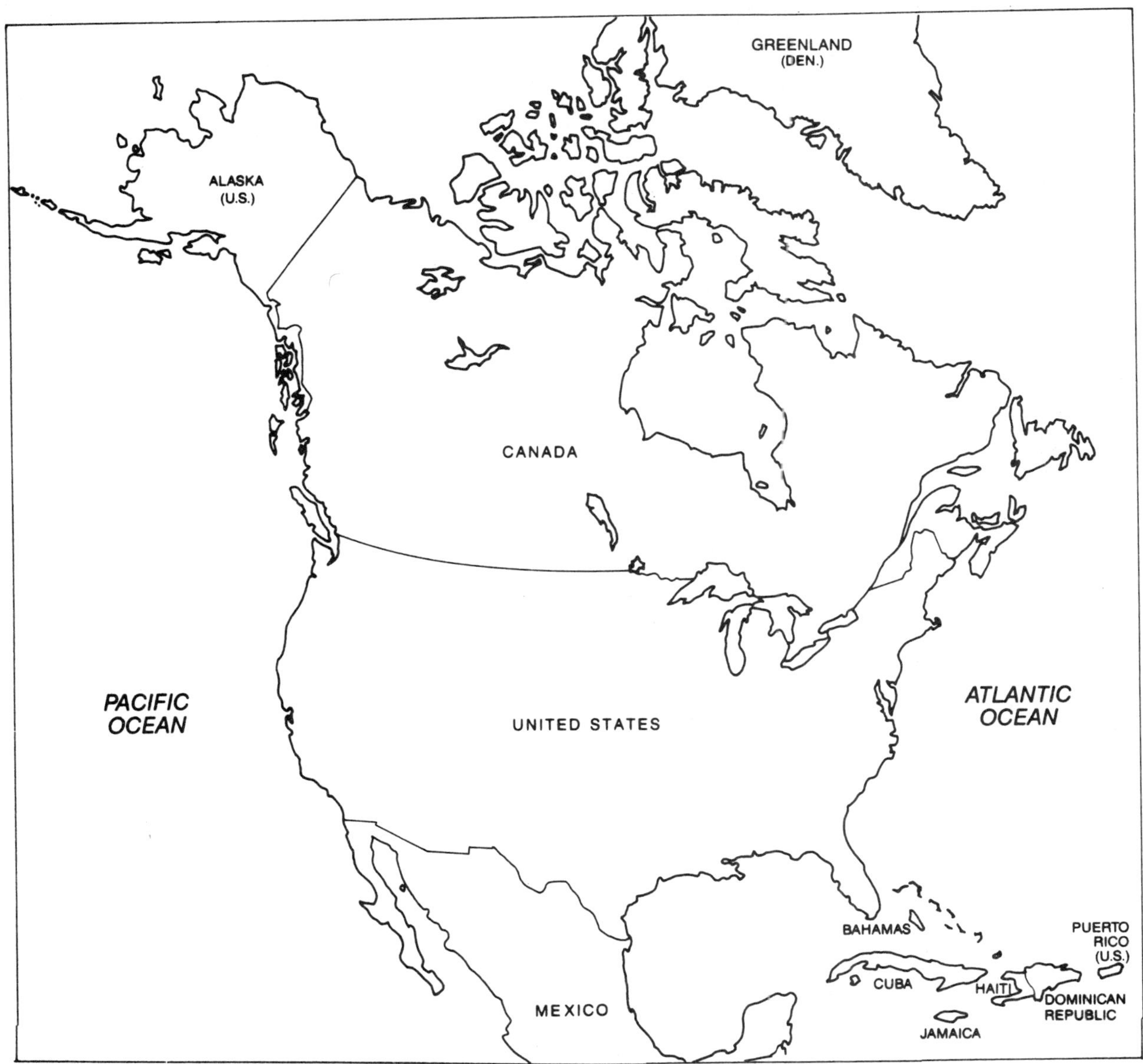

LOCAL COLORS

Name ____________________

Colors on maps can be very useful. They help to separate different states and countries. Look at this map of the United States. Margaret Mabel Mapmaker is supposed to color it in. Unfortunately, she has misplaced her chart of states and colors.

While she looks for it, you can find the information on page 67. Use it to color in the map below.

Name ______________________________

LOCAL COLORS

The chart below shows the colors Margaret Mabel should use to color in the United States map on page 66. Margaret Mabel still hasn't found her copy of the chart, so you will have to do it for her. Read the chart below. Using crayons or colored pencils, follow its instructions to color the states on the map on page 66. When you finish, you should see that each state is a different color from the states it borders.

Colors	Yellow	Blue	Orange	Pink	Green
States	Washington Utah Oklahoma South Dakota Illinois Mississippi South Carolina New York Hawaii Delaware	California Wyoming Texas Iowa Kentucky Alabama North Carolina Massachusetts	Idaho Arizona Nebraska Wisconsin Louisiana Tennessee Ohio Connecticut Maryland New Hampshire Alaska	Oregon Colorado North Dakota Missouri Michigan West Virginia Georgia New Jersey Vermont Rhode Island	Nevada Montana New Mexico Kansas Minnesota Arkansas Indiana Florida Virginia Pennsylvania Maine

Name ___________________________

NAME THAT STATE!

The whole country is tuned in to the newest TV quiz show, *Name That State!* It's fun to watch famous people try to top each other as they answer questions about the states of the United States. Now you can play too. Read the questions below. Write your answers on the lines provided. If you need help, consult a map of the United States.

1. Four state names end with the letter *o*. Three of them are Colorado, Ohio, and Idaho. What's the fourth? NAME THAT STATE! ___________________________
2. One state has an *x* in the exact middle of its name. Which one is it? NAME THAT STATE! ___________________________
3. One state's name ends in three vowels. (Vowels are the letters *a, e, i, o, u.*) Which one is it? NAME THAT STATE! ___________________________
4. Four state names begin with the word *New*. Three of them are New Hampshire, New Jersey, and New York. What's the fourth? NAME THAT STATE! ___________________________
5. Two states have four *s*'s in their names. One is Mississippi. What's the other one? NAME THAT STATE! ___________________________
6. One state has a *z* in the exact middle of its name. Which one is it? NAME THAT STATE! ___________________________
7. Two state names end with the letter *y*. One is New Jersey. What's the other one? NAME THAT STATE! ___________________________
8. Only one state name begins with the letter *D*. Which one is it? NAME THAT STATE! ___________________________
9. Five states have direction words as parts of their names. Four of them are North Carolina, South Carolina, North Dakota, and South Dakota. What's the fifth? NAME THAT STATE! ___________________________
10. Two state names contain the letters *k, a, n, s, a, s*. One is Kansas. What's the other one? NAME THAT STATE! ___________________________

Name ______________________

A CAPITAL CAMPAIGN

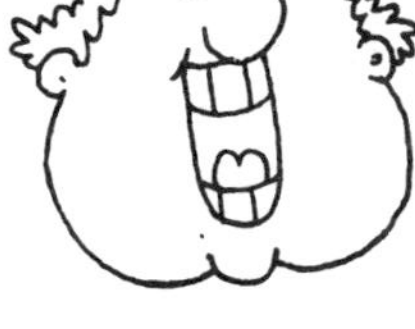

You have just been appointed campaign manager for Windy Boggs, a presidential candidate. Windy has a list of 10 state capitals that he plans to visit. Unfortunately, he doesn't know which states they are the capitals of!

Look at the map of the United States below. It shows the capitals of every state. Use this map to complete page 70.

★ state capital
✪ national capital

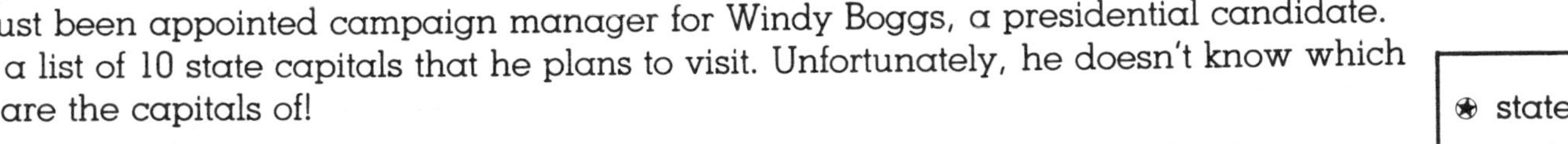

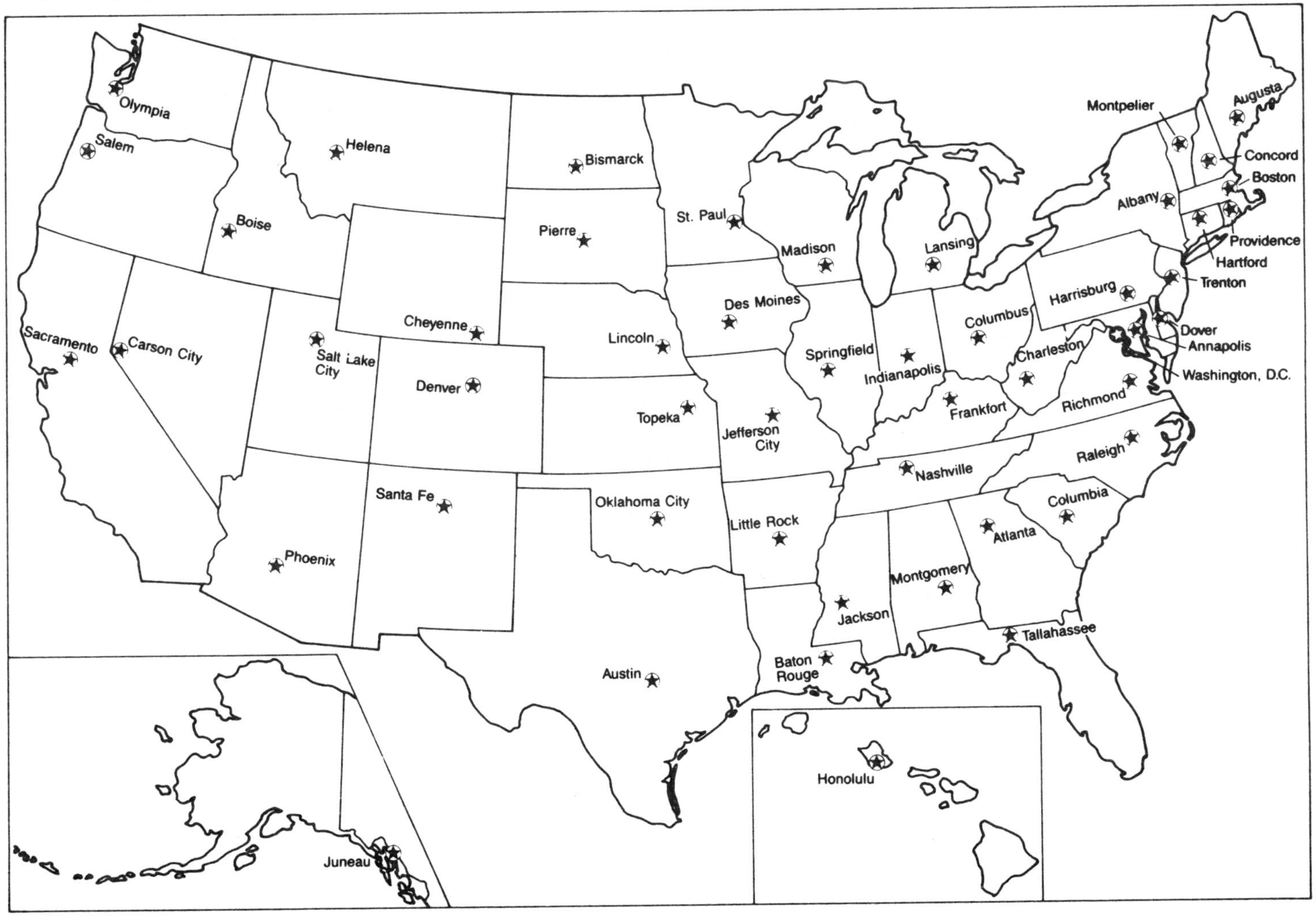

Name ______________________________

A CAPITAL CAMPAIGN

Read Windy Boggs's list of state capitals below. Then look at the map of the United States on page 69. On the map, find each state capital listed. If you can identify the state by its outline, write its name on the list on the line provided. Otherwise, look up the state's name in an atlas and then write it on the list.

1. St. Paul, ______________________________
2. Trenton, ______________________________
3. Columbus, ______________________________
4. Little Rock, ______________________________
5. Denver, ______________________________
6. Richmond, ______________________________
7. Baton Rouge, ______________________________
8. Atlanta, ______________________________
9. Concord, ______________________________
10. Salt Lake City, ______________________________

LET'S GET PHYSICAL

Name ____________________

Rhoda Rails, a member of the Happy Wanderers, is planning a train tour of the United States. Rhoda's favorite sports are boating, mountain climbing, and dune-buggy racing. Naturally, she wants to know where she can find rivers and lakes, mountains, and deserts, so she can enjoy these pastimes. She is going to study a physical map of the United States to find out what she wants to know.

Look at Rhoda's map below. It shows what the surface of the earth looks like. Notice the map symbols. Then use information from this map to complete page 72.

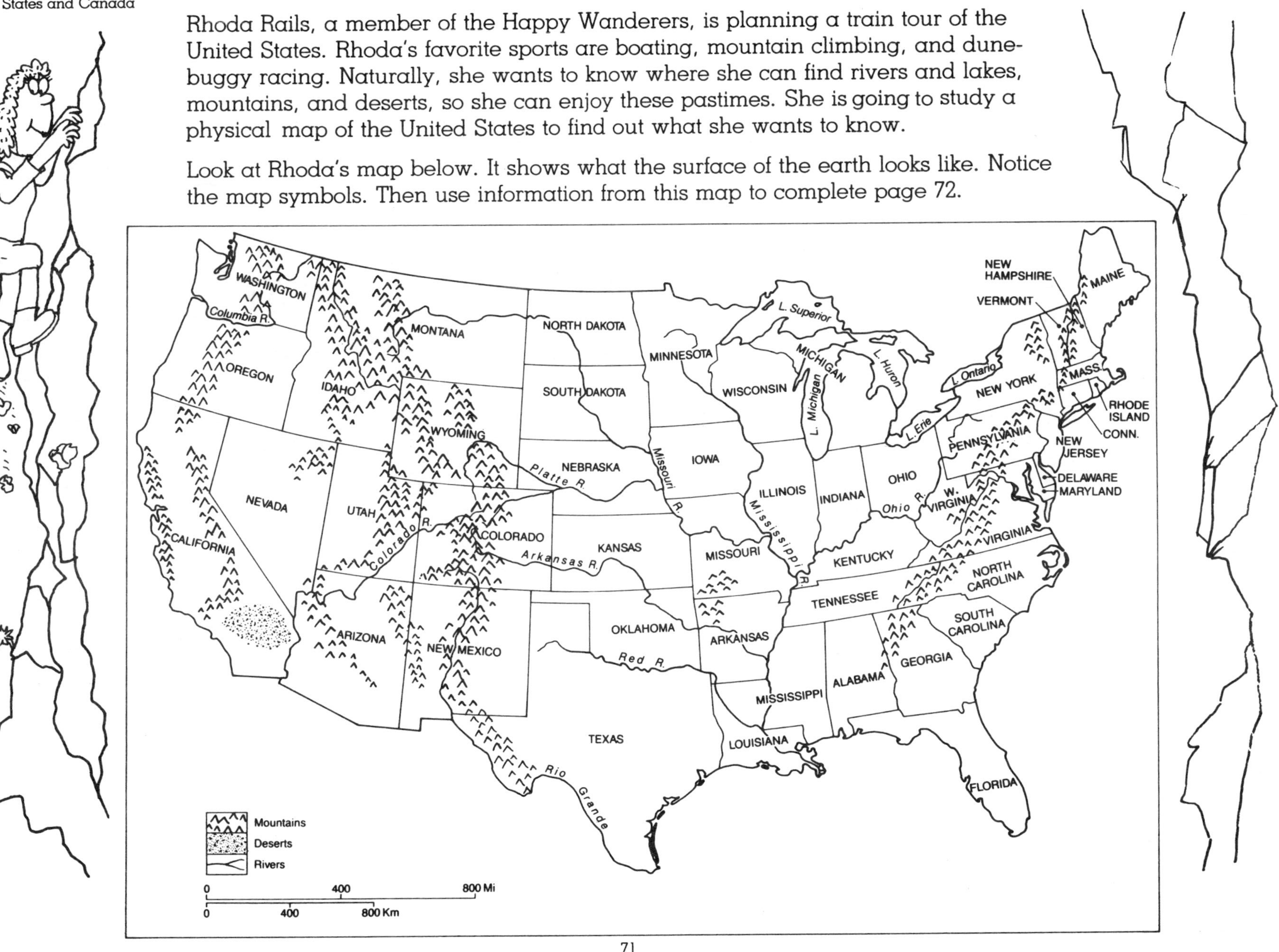

Name ________________________________

LET'S GET PHYSICAL

Look at the physical map of the United States on page 71. Then read the statements below. Use the map to figure out whether a statement is true or false. Then draw a check (✓) on the line provided in either the True or the False column.

	True	False
1. There are no mountain ranges in the state of California.	____	____
2. There are mountains in the western states of Idaho, Wyoming, and Colorado.	____	____
3. The Rio Grande forms part of Arizona's border.	____	____
4. One of the lakes bordering Michigan is Lake Tarpon.	____	____
5. Florida is a fairly mountainous state.	____	____
6. The Missouri River runs through the state of Missouri. It also runs through North and South Dakota.	____	____
7. The Mississippi River forms a boundary line between Iowa and Nebraska.	____	____
8. The Ohio River forms a boundary line between Indiana and Kentucky.	____	____
9. A mountain range runs along the western borders of Virginia and North Carolina.	____	____
10. A large desert area is located in southern California.	____	____

Name ______________________

THE MISSING STATES

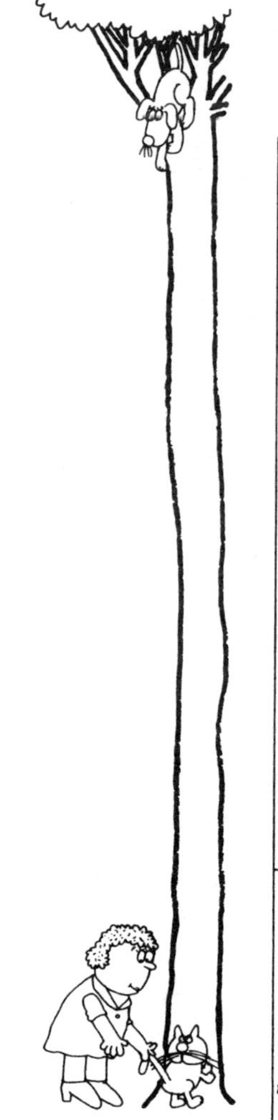

Aunt Mavis Mapmaker was making a map of the United States. Unfortunately, before she could finish, a ruckus broke out. Aunt Mavis's cat, Mitzi, attacked the dog next door and chased it up a tree. While Aunt Mavis rescues the dog, you can finish the map for her.

Look at the map below. The names of 10 states are missing. Write the state names on the lines provided. Use a map of the United States or an atlas to help you.

WASHINGTON
OREGON
CALIFORNIA
NEVADA
IDAHO
WYOMING
COLORADO
NEW MEXICO
NORTH DAKOTA
SOUTH DAKOTA
NEBRASKA
OKLAHOMA
MINNESOTA
WISCONSIN
MICHIGAN
ILLINOIS
INDIANA
MISSOURI
ARKANSAS
LOUISIANA
MISSISSIPPI
ALABAMA
TENNESSEE
KENTUCKY
W VIRGINIA
PENNSYLVANIA
NEW YORK
VERMONT
NEW HAMPSHIRE
MASS.
RHODE ISLAND
CONN.
NEW JERSEY
DELAWARE
MARYLAND
NORTH CAROLINA
SOUTH CAROLINA
FLORIDA
ALASKA
HAWAII

Name ______________________

SHORT STATES

Look at the crossword puzzle below. Then read the clues. The clues are some of the common abbreviations for state names that may be used on maps. At the right is an alphabetical list of all 50 states. Use it to help you complete the puzzle.

When you finish, look at the letters you wrote in the shaded squares. Unscramble them and write them on the lines at the bottom of the page to find what all 50 states are part of.

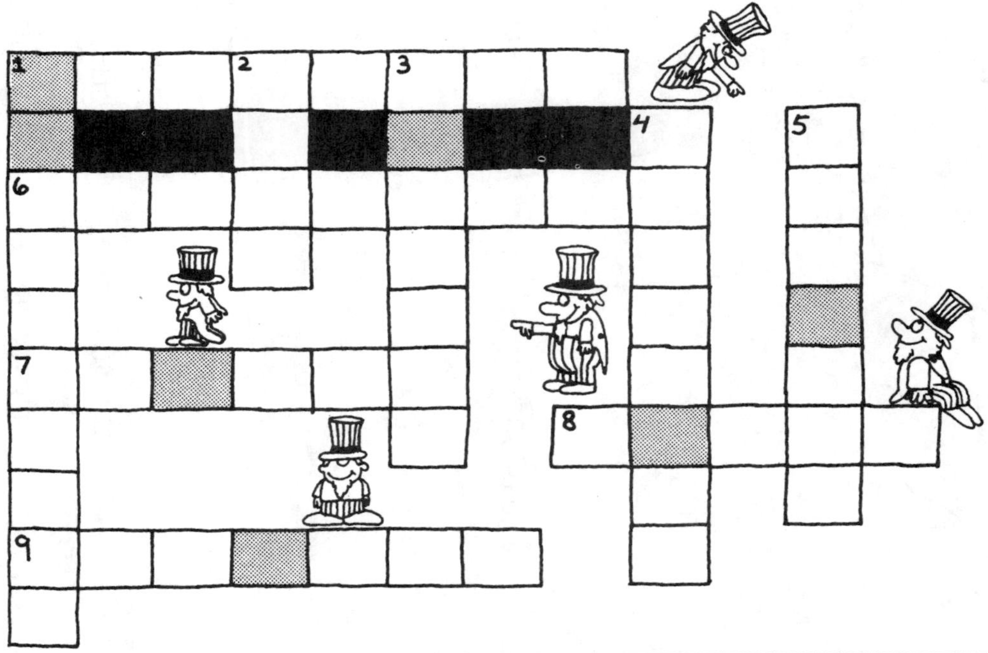

Alabama	Louisiana	Ohio
Alaska	Maine	Oklahoma
Arizona	Maryland	Oregon
Arkansas	Massachusetts	Pennsylvania
California	Michigan	Rhode Island
Colorado	Minnesota	South Carolina
Connecticut	Mississippi	South Dakota
Delaware	Missouri	Tennessee
Florida	Montana	Texas
Georgia	Nebraska	Utah
Hawaii	Nevada	Vermont
Idaho	New Hampshire	Virginia
Illinois	New Jersey	Washington
Indiana	New Mexico	West Virginia
Iowa	New York	Wisconsin
Kansas	North Carolina	Wyoming
Kentucky	North Dakota	

Across	**Down**
1. Colo.	1. Calif.
6. La.	2. Oh.
7. Oreg.	3. Ariz.
8. Me.	4. Md.
9. Ind.	5. Vt.

The 50 states are part of ___ ___ ___ ___ ___ ___ ___.

Name ____________________

IT'S ABOUT TIME!

Look at an atlas, almanac, or United States map displayed in your classroom to help you answer the questions below. Write your answers on the lines provided.

1. Which time zone is Mississippi in? ____________________
2. Name the three states which are completely within the Pacific Time Zone.

   ____
3. Which state is within four separate time zones?

   ____
4. When it is 7 P.M. in Wichita, Kansas, what time is it in Cheyenne, Wyoming?

   ____
5. When it is 10 A.M. in San Diego, California, what time is it in Denver, Colo.?

   ____
6. When it is 4 P.M. in Harrisburg, Pennsylvania, what time is it in Billings, Montana?

   ____
7. When it is 2 A.M. in Spokane, Washington, what time is it in Fairbanks, Alaska?

   ____
8. When it is midnight in Charlotte, North Carolina, what time is it in Eugene, Oregon?

   ____
9. When it is 5 P.M. in Juneau, Alaska, what time is it in Hilo, Hawaii?

   ____
10. When it is 3 A.M. in Honolulu, Hawaii, what time is it in Anchorage, Alaska?

    ____

Name ______________________

ANIMALS AT HOME

The United States is home to many kinds of animals. Below is a *habitat* map, which shows where five of these kinds of animals live. Look at the map and the symbols. Use this information to complete page 77.

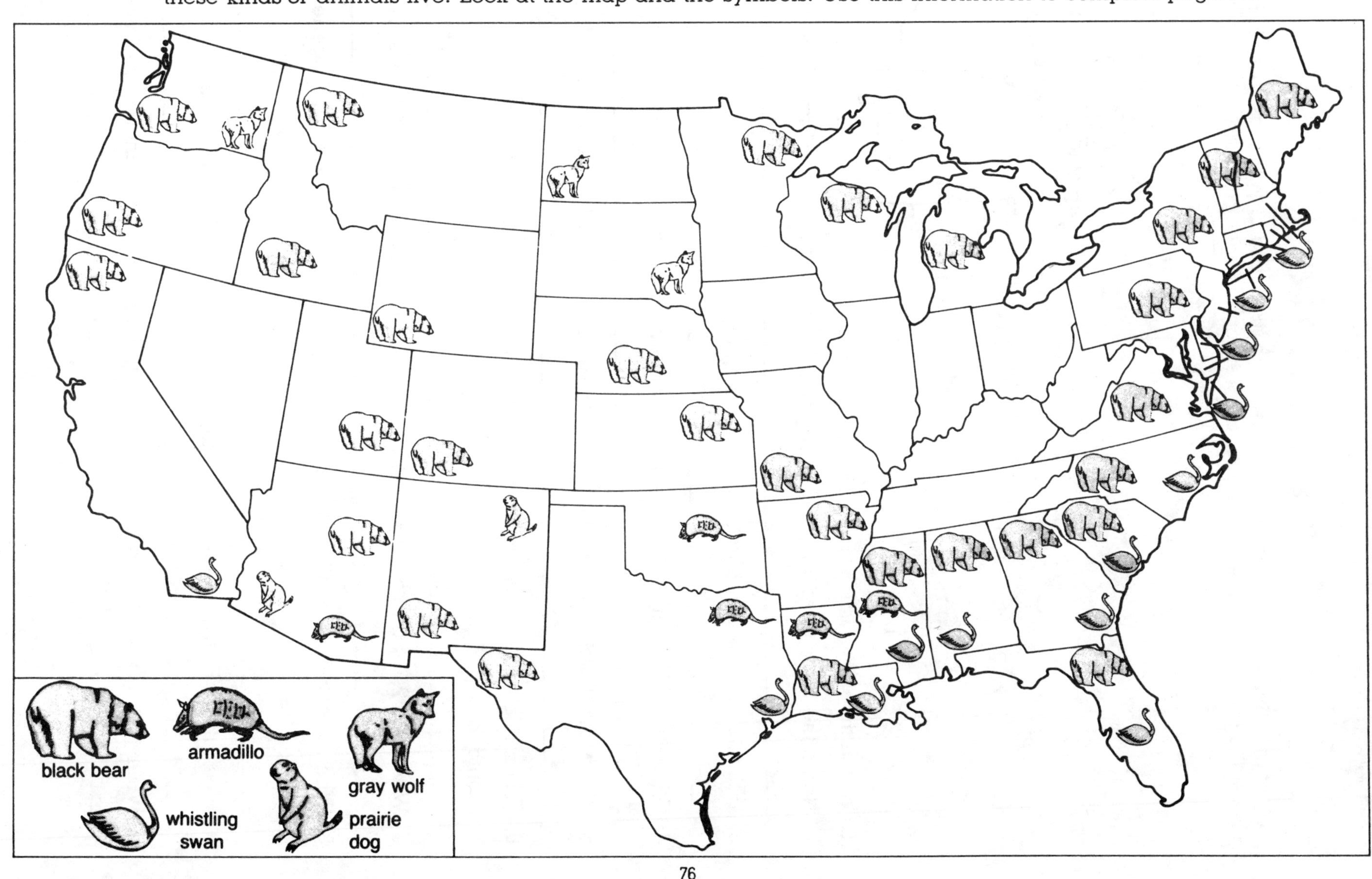

Name ______________________

ANIMALS AT HOME

Look at the habitat map and map symbols on page 76. Use this information to answer the questions below. Write your answers on the lines provided. If necessary, use an atlas to help you.

1. In how many states do armadillos live? ______________________
2. According to this map, which animal lives in only two states? ______________________
3. Where do gray wolves live, in the northern or southern part of the United States? ______________________
4. Where do <u>most</u> whistling swans live, in the eastern or western part of the United States? ______________________
5. Of the five animals shown, which one lives in the greatest number of states? ______________________
6. Of the five animals shown, which two live in California? ______________________
7. Of the five animals shown, which three live in Texas? ______________________
8. Of the five animals shown, which two live in Florida? ______________________
9. Of the five animals shown, which one lives in Maine? ______________________
10. Of the five animals shown, do any live in your state? ______________________
    If so, which one(s)? ______________________

Name ______________________________

WEATHER, WHETHER OR NOT

Weather maps tell us what kind of weather to expect. By means of symbols, they show the temperature, wind direction, storms, and other weather conditions over a given area.

Look at the sample weather map of the United States below. Study the weather symbols beneath it. Use this information to complete page 79.

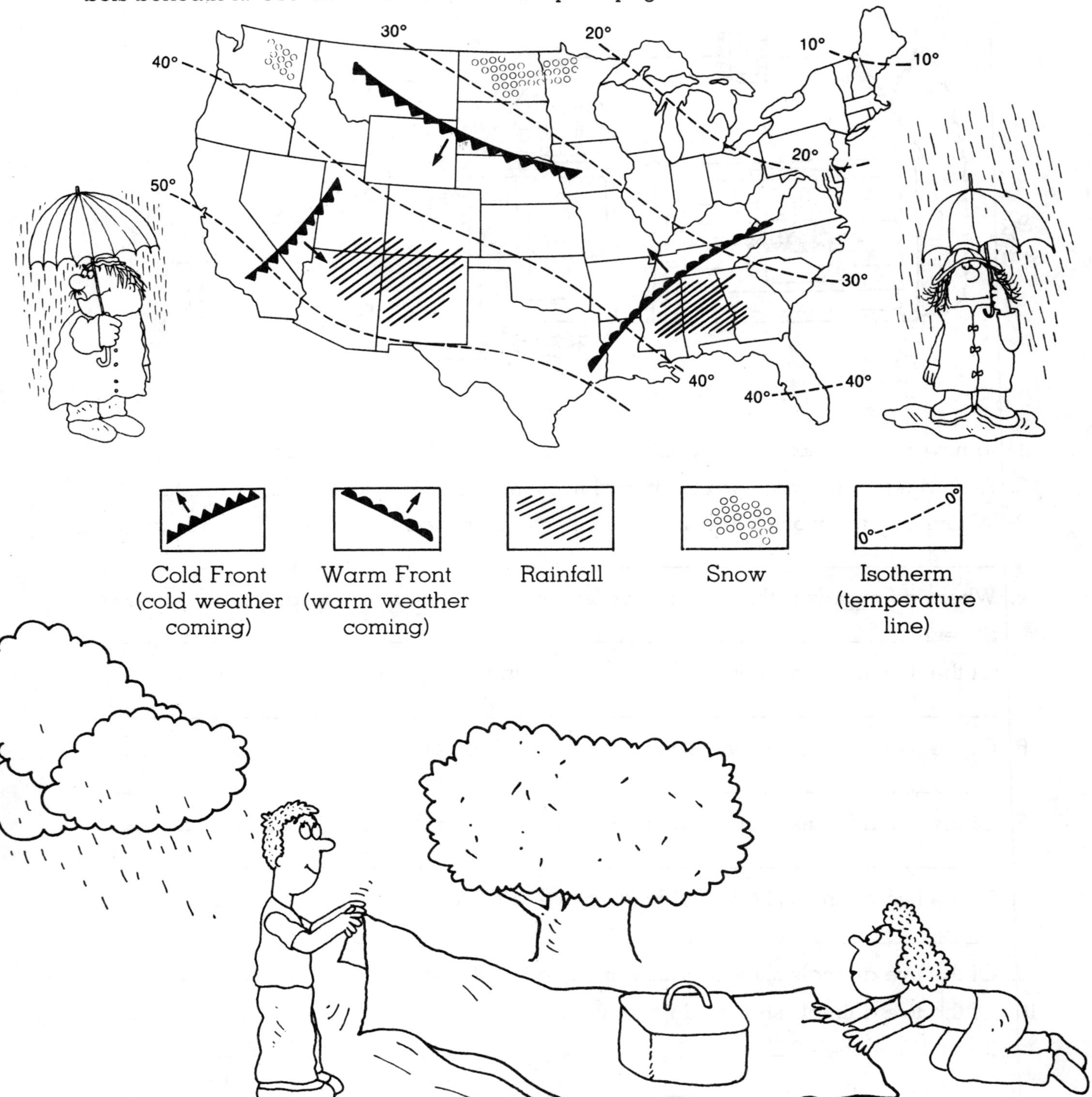

Name ____________________

WEATHER, WHETHER OR NOT

Look at the sample weather map and the weather symbols on page 78. Then read the instructions below to turn this outline map into a weather map of the United States.

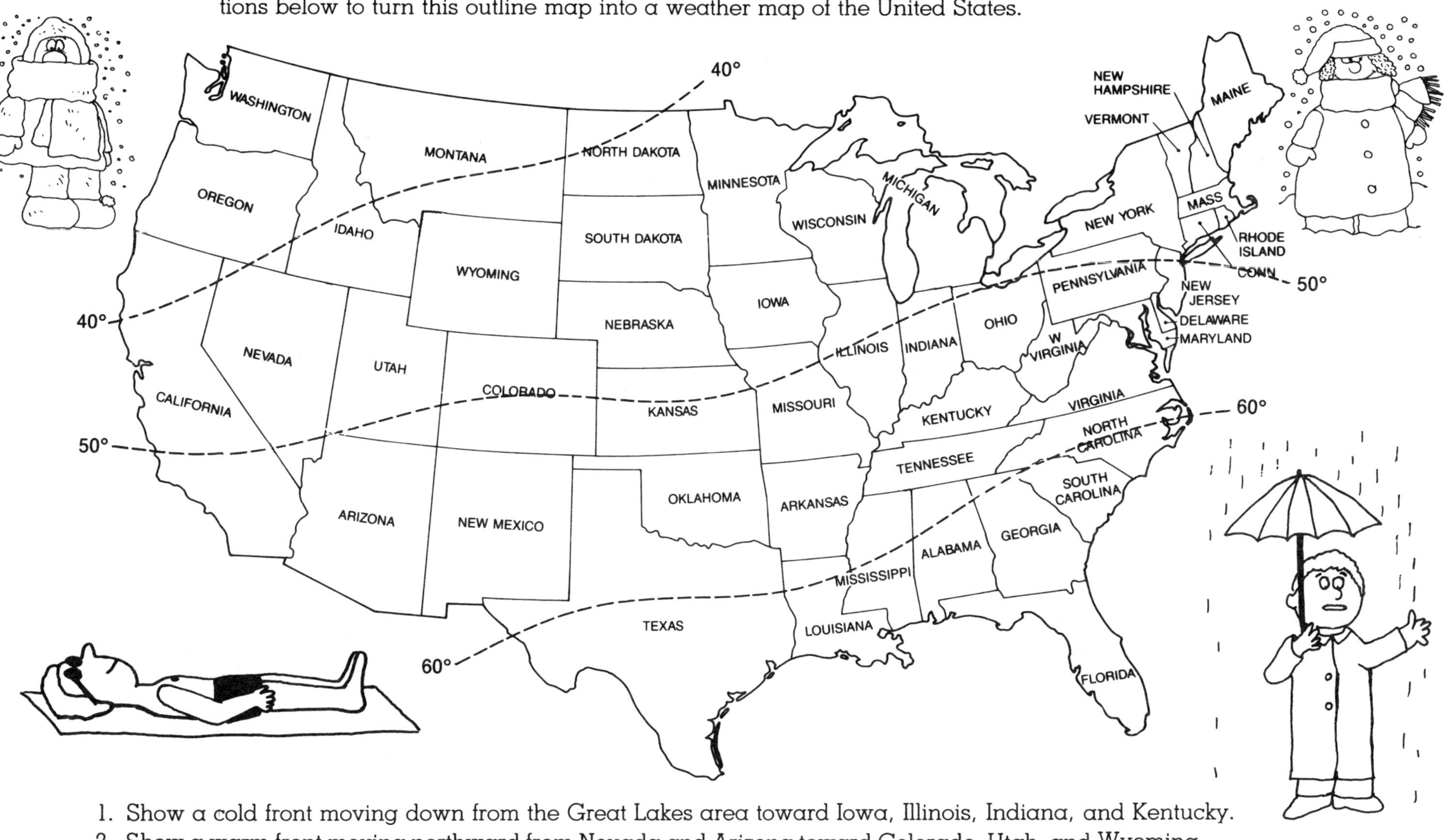

1. Show a cold front moving down from the Great Lakes area toward Iowa, Illinois, Indiana, and Kentucky.
2. Show a warm front moving northward from Nevada and Arizona toward Colorado, Utah, and Wyoming.
3. Show a heavy snowstorm covering the northern states of Washington, Idaho, Montana, and North Dakota.
4. It's raining in the South! Show rainfall over these states: Alabama, Tennessee, and Georgia.

Name ______________________

WE, THE PEOPLE

According to the 1980 United States Census Bureau figures, which keeps track of population changes, many Americans have relocated in recent years. This map shows the expected percentage (%) of population gain (+) and loss (–) by the year 2000. Look at the map below and read the percentages for each state. Use this information to complete page 81.

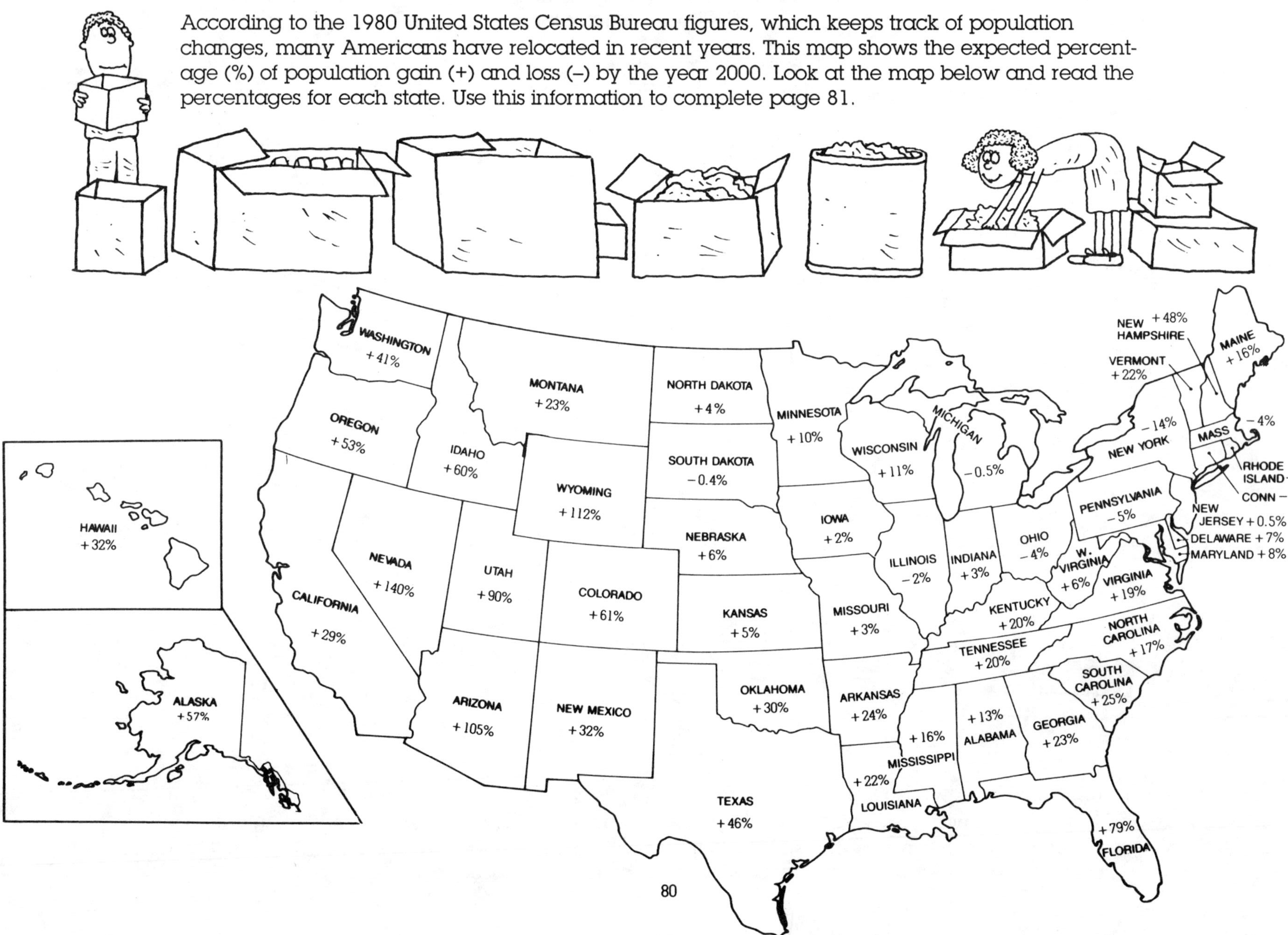

Name ______________________

WE, THE PEOPLE

Look at the map on page 80. Use it to answer the questions below. Write your answers on the lines provided.

Cross-Country Van Lines

1. What percentage of population gain or loss is expected for the following states?
   a. Wisconsin ____
   b. Missouri ____
   c. Idaho ____
   d. Georgia ____
   e. Oregon ____
   f. Massachusetts ____
   g. Pennsylvania ____
   h. Ohio ____
   i. Illinois ____
   j. Connecticut ____
2. According to the map, which state is expected to have the biggest gain in population and what will the percentage of that gain be? ______________________
3. Which state is expected to have the biggest loss in population and what will the percentage of that loss be? ______________________
4. Look at the map again. In general, which part of the country will be gaining the greatest percentage of people, the east or the west? ______________________

CANADIAN CITIES GAME

On the chalkboard, write the information in the box at the bottom of the page. Tell your students that you are going to distribute copies of a map of Canada, which shows the cities listed on the board. Explain that they are to use the map key—the letters and numbers along the margins of the map—to locate the cities.

If necessary, demonstrate how to use a map key. Write the letters A, B, C and the numbers 1, 2, 3 on the chalkboard as shown. With your fingers, show how to move one finger across from a letter and another finger down or up from a number until both fingers meet. Tell students that somewhere around this point, they will find the city they are looking for.

Distribute copies of page 83. As students locate each city, they are to write its number next to it on the map. Once they have located and numbered all the cities listed on the board, they are to raise their hands.

Check each student's map. The first student to correctly locate and number all the cities listed wins the game.

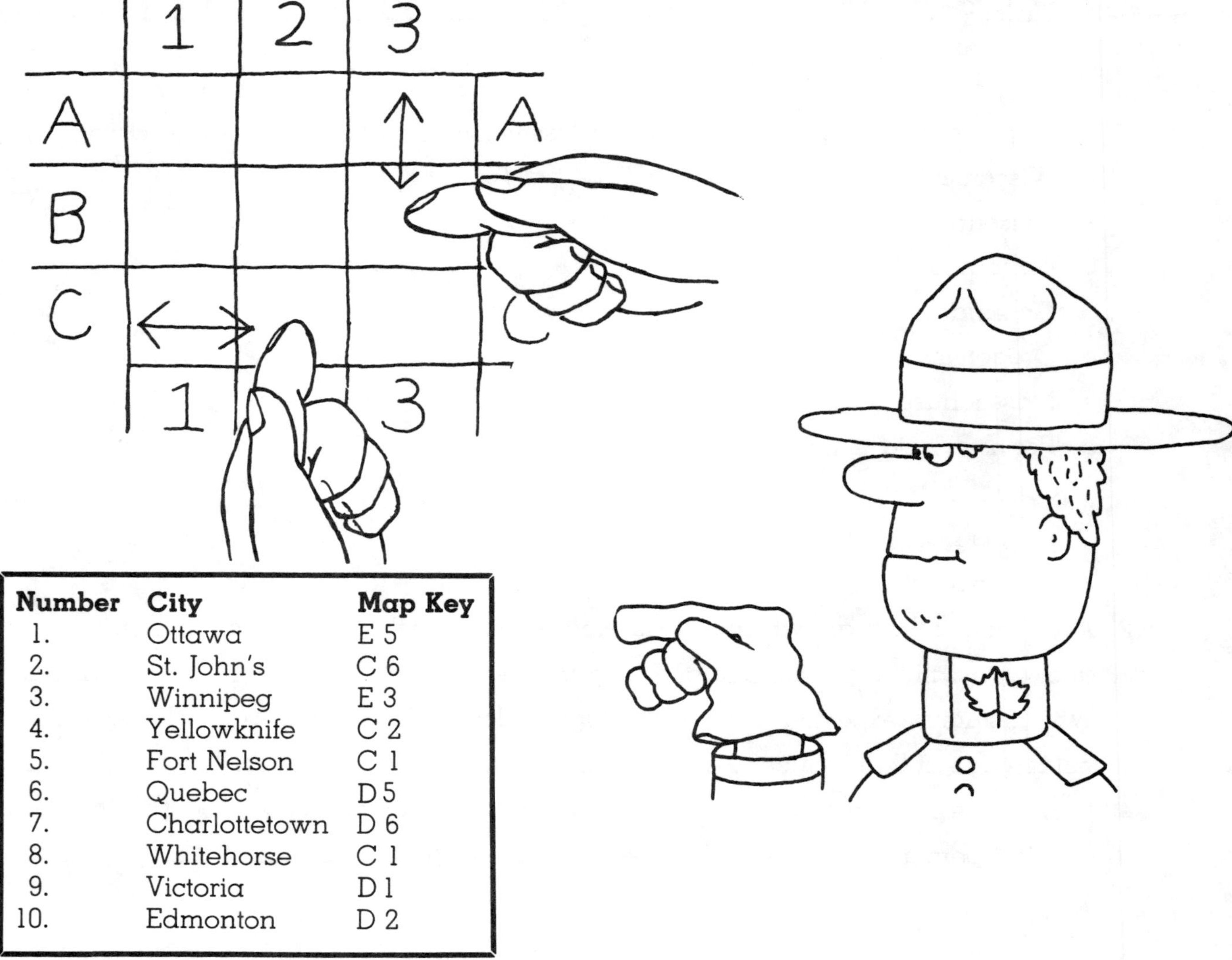

Number	City	Map Key
1.	Ottawa	E 5
2.	St. John's	C 6
3.	Winnipeg	E 3
4.	Yellowknife	C 2
5.	Fort Nelson	C 1
6.	Quebec	D 5
7.	Charlottetown	D 6
8.	Whitehorse	C 1
9.	Victoria	D 1
10.	Edmonton	D 2

Name ______________________

CANADIAN CITIES GAME

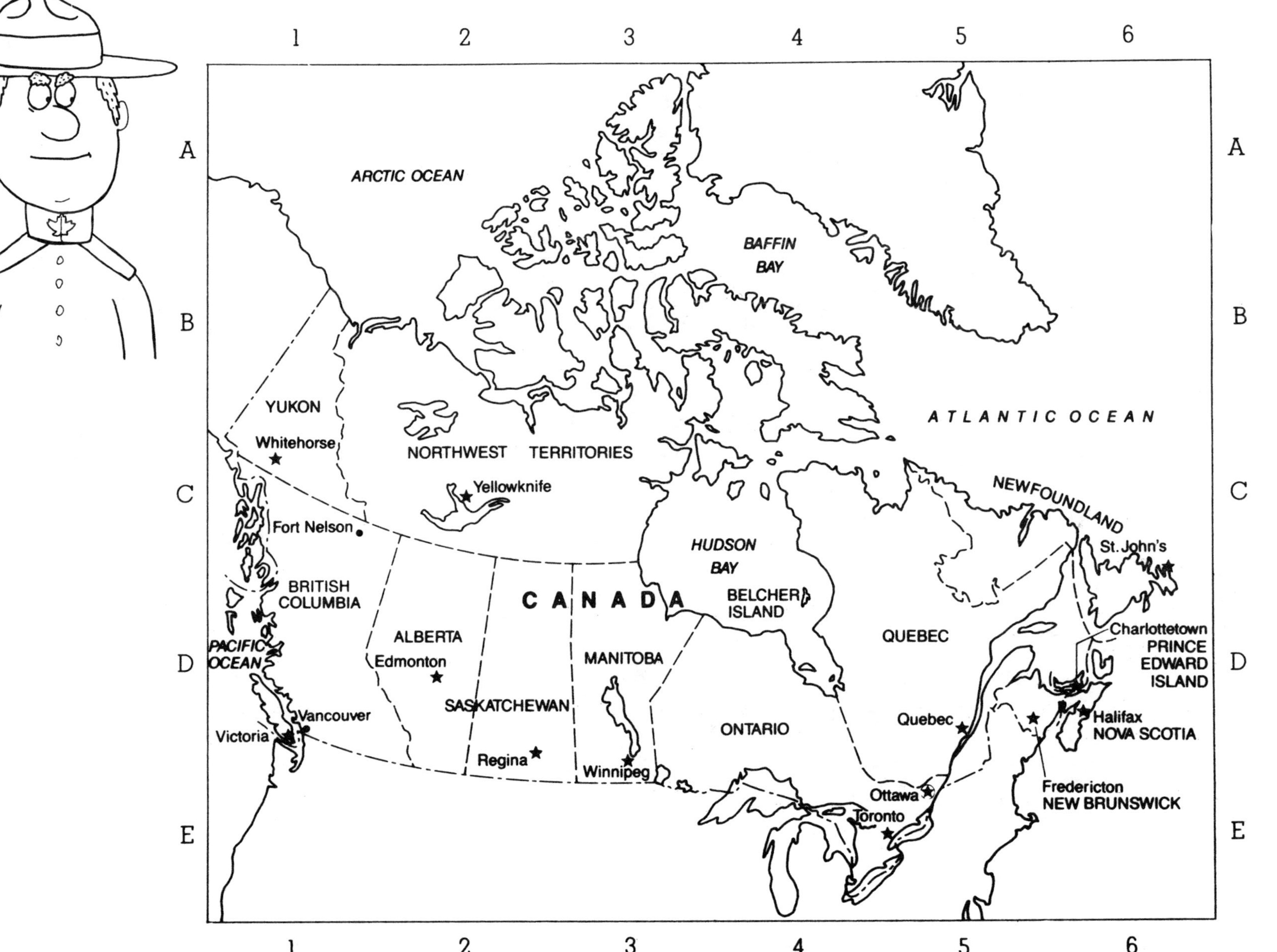

Answer Sheet for *United States and Canada*—Section 4

Colorful Countries—page 65

Answers will vary. Bordering countries should be different colors. Alaska and Puerto Rico should be the same color as the United States.

Local Colors—page 66

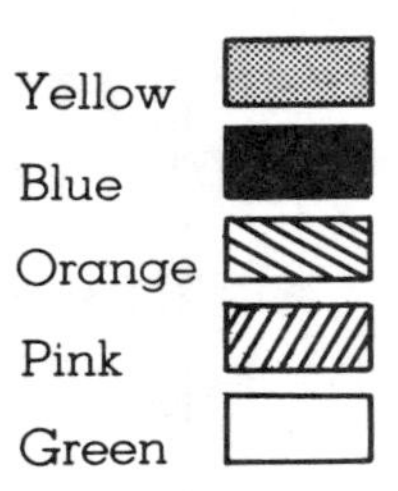

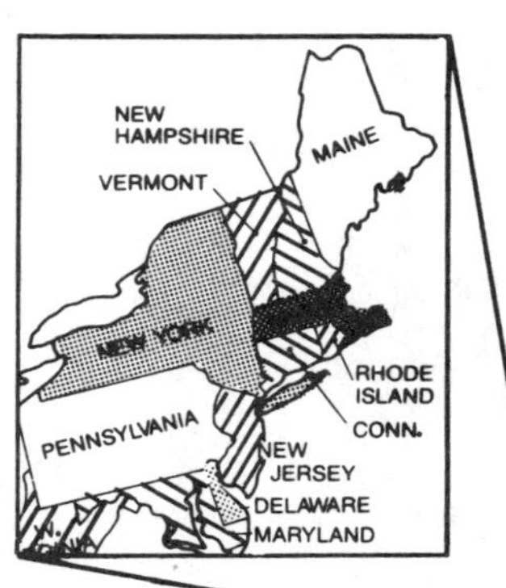

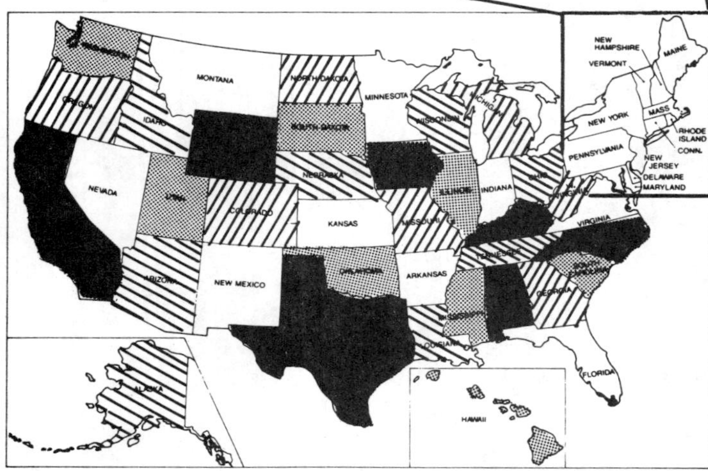

Name That State! - page 68

1. New Mexico
2. Texas
3. Hawaii
4. New Mexico
5. Massachusetts
6. Arizona
7. Kentucky
8. Delaware
9. West Virginia
10. Arkansas

A Capital Campaign - Page 70

1. Minnesota
2. New Jersey
3. Ohio
4. Arkansas
5. Colorado
6. Virginia
7. Louisiana
8. Georgia
9. New Hampshire
10. Utah

Lets Get Physical—page 72

1. false
2. true
3. false
4. false
5. false
6. true
7. false
8. true
9. true
10. true

The Missing States—page 73

Short States—page 74

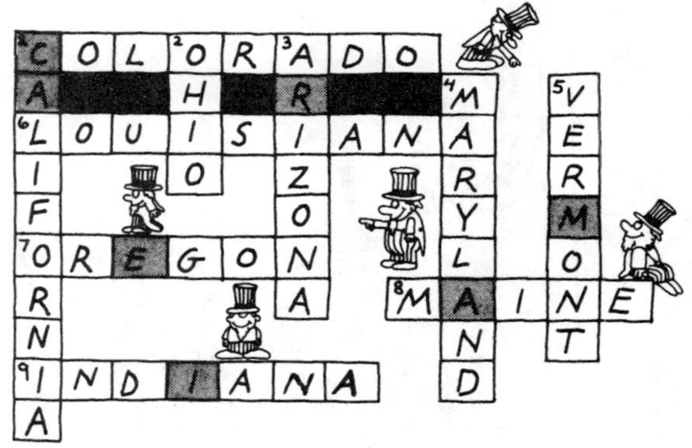

AMERICA

Answer Sheet for *United States and Canada*—Section 4

It's About Time!—page 75

1. Central
2. Washington, Nevada, California
3. Alaska
4. 6 P.M.
5. 11 A.M.
6. 2 P.M.
7. midnight
8. 9 P.M.
9. 4 P.M.
10. 3 A.M.

Animals at Home—page 77

1. five
2. the prairie dog
3. northern
4. eastern
5. the black bear
6. the black bear and the whistling swan
7. the black bear, the armadillo, and the whistling swan
8. the black bear and the whistling swan
9. the black bear
10. Answers will vary.

Weather, Whether or Not—page 79

We, the People—page 81

1. a. + 11%
   b. + 3%
   c. + 60%
   d. + 23%
   e. + 53%
   f. − 4%
   g. − 5%
   h. − 4%
   i. − 2%
   j. − 2%
2. Nevada; 140%
3. New York; 14%
4. the west

Canadian Cities Game—page 83

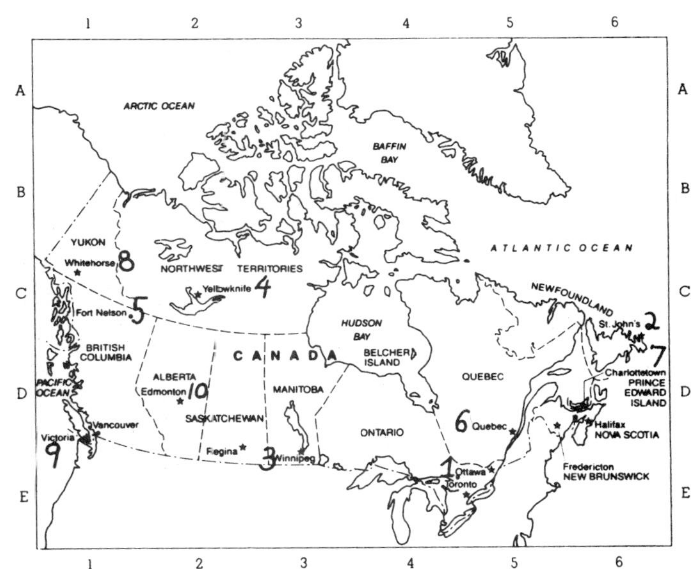

Name ______________________________

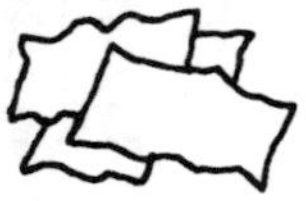

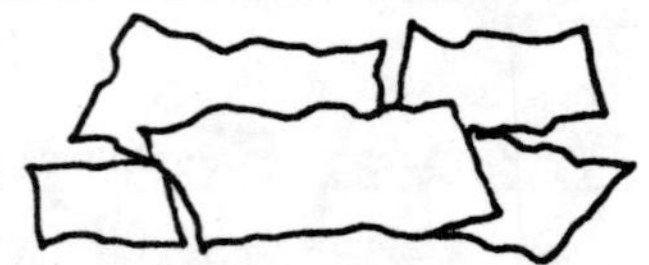

COUNTRIES SHAPE UP

Margaret Mabel Mapmaker is baby-sitting for her younger brother, Little Map. Unfortunately, while Margaret Mabel was watching TV, Little Map peeled the labels off a bunch of maps. These maps need to be sent out to the printer as soon as their mother comes home.

Help put the labels back on the maps. First look below at the outline maps of different countries. Then read the list of country names in the box. With the help of an atlas, match the maps with their correct names. Write the names on the lines provided.

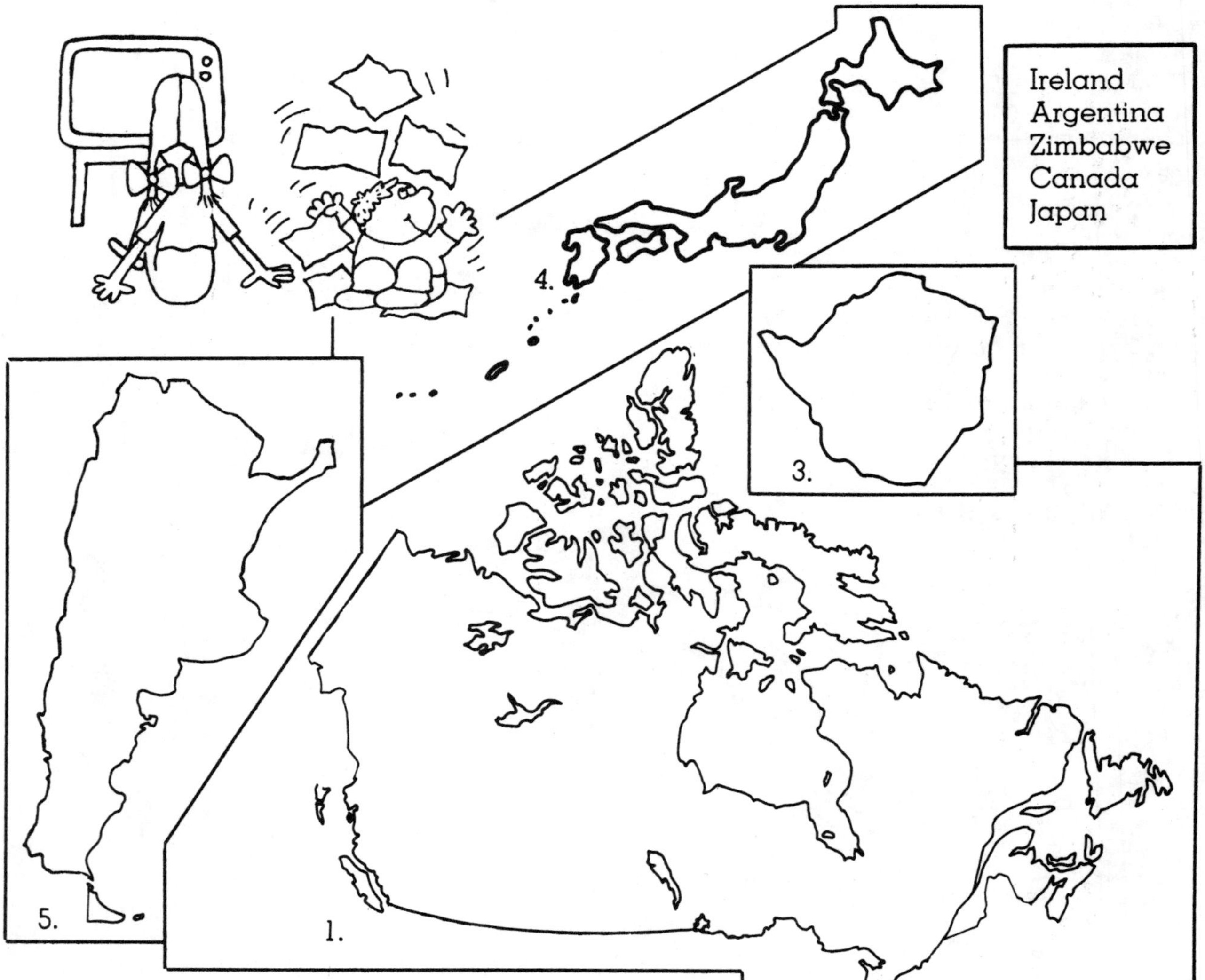

Ireland
Argentina
Zimbabwe
Canada
Japan

4.

3.

5.

1.

2.

1. ______________________________
2. ______________________________
3. ______________________________
4. ______________________________
5. ______________________________

Name ______________________

MAKE MINE MEXICO!

Con Vertible, a member of the Happy Wanderers, is planning an automobile trip through Mexico. Con, who is also an amateur artist, is looking for some spectacular scenery to paint. Therefore, he'd like to know the location of the country's mountains and waterways. He'd also like to know where he can enter Mexico from the United States.

Use the physical map of Mexico below to find the information Con needs. Write your answers on the lines provided.

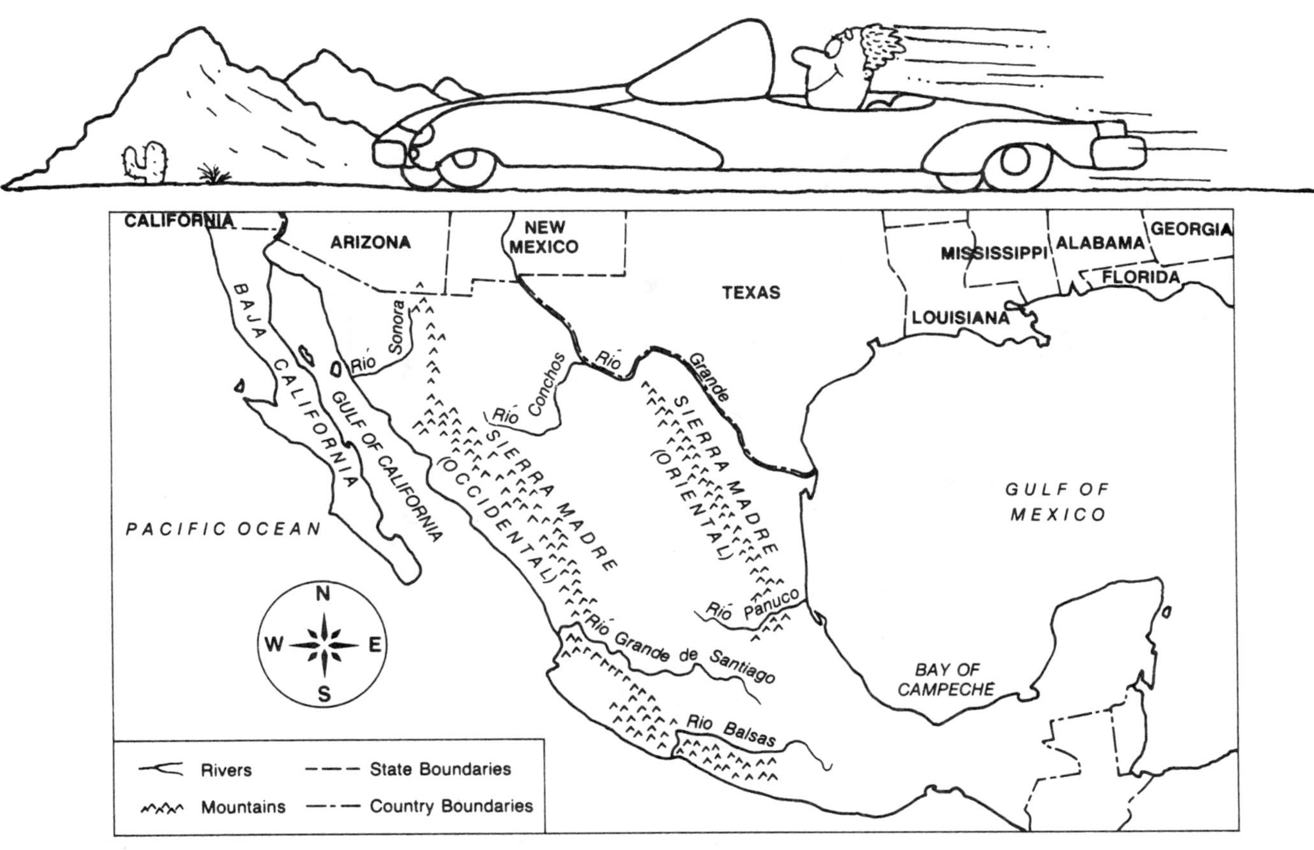

1. Name the four states that border Mexico on the north.

   ______________ ______________ ______________ ______________

2. What river forms part of the boundary between Mexico and the United States?

   ____

3. A gulf and a bay border Mexico on its eastern shore. Name both.

   Gulf of ______________ Bay of ______________

4. Two mighty mountain ranges extend through Mexico. Name them.

   ______________________ ______________________

5. What is the name of the long narrow peninsula that stretches along Mexico's western shore? ______________________

Name ____________________

UNCLE MAC'S MAP

Uncle Mac Mapmaker is supposed to be adding lines of latitude and longitude to a map. Unfortunately, he wandered into the kitchen to find something to eat and forgot to come back. Now you will have to finish the job for him.

Look at the map below. Draw lines of latitude and longitude on it by following the instructions on page 89.

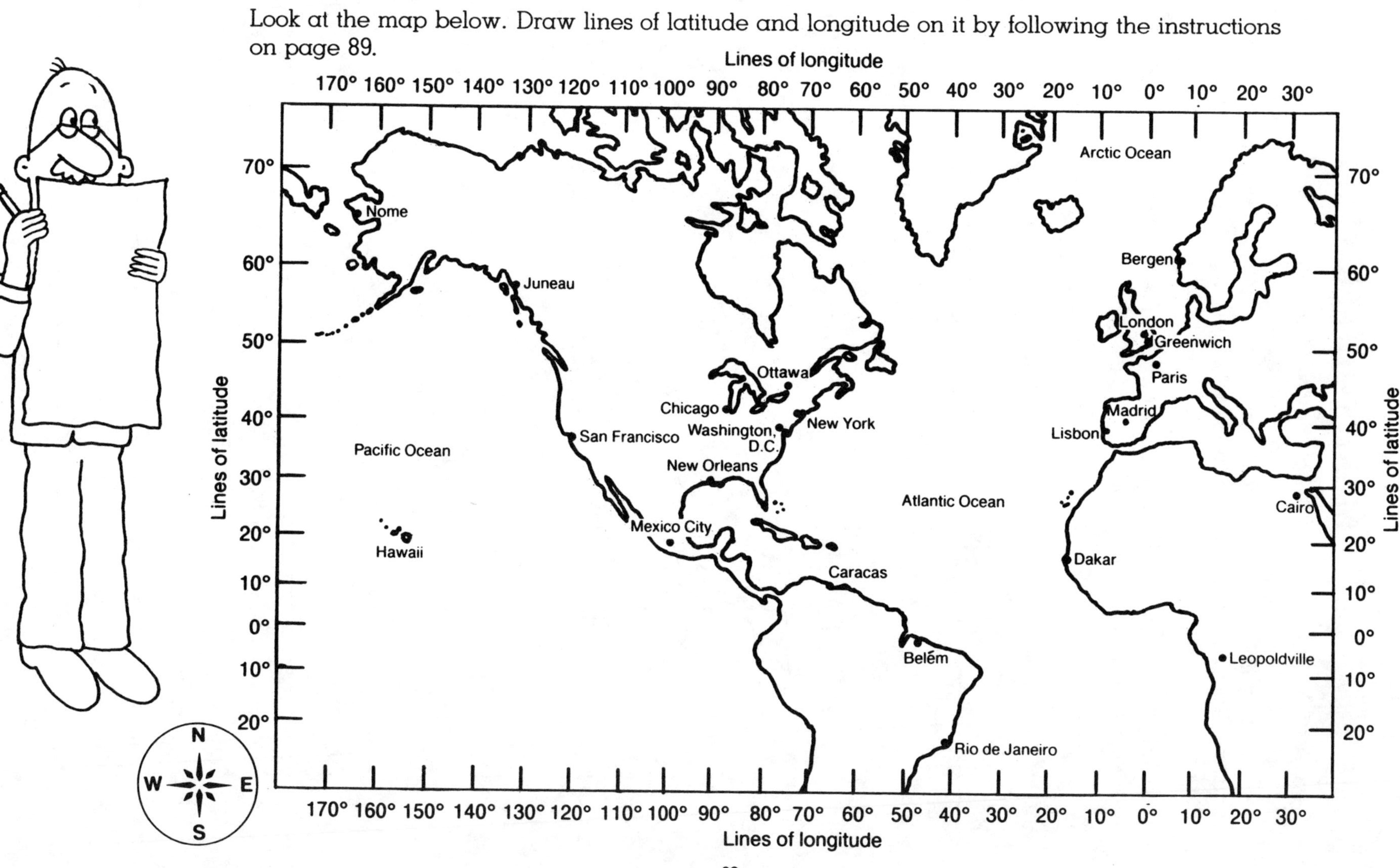

Name ______________________

UNCLE MAC'S MAP

Look at the map on page 88. Notice the marks around the margin. These are guide points. Use them and a ruler and pencil to help you complete the map as follows:

1. The equator is at zero degree latitude. To draw it, find the two points marked 0° latitude (lat.) and draw a line between them. Write the word *equator* above the line.
2. Using the rest of the guide points on the left and right sides of the map, draw in all the other horizontal lines of latitude above and below the equator.
3. The prime meridian is at zero degree longitude. To draw it, find the two points marked 0° longitude (long.) and draw a line between them. Write the words *prime meridian* along the line.
4. Using the rest of the guide points on the top and bottom of the map, draw in all the other vertical lines of longitude on either side of the prime meridian.

Now look at the area of the map north of the equator and west of the prime meridian. Read the coordinates below. (*Coordinates* are the degree numbers that show where lines of latitude and lines of longitude intersect.) Locate these points on the map. On the line provided, write the name of the city closest to each point.

1. 30° lat., 90° long. ______________________
2. 70° lat., 160° long. ______________________
3. 40° lat., 70° long. ______________________
4. 60° lat., 130° long. ______________________
5. 40° lat., 120° long. ______________________

Name ______________________________

SCRAMBLED COUNTRIES

Eastward across the Atlantic Ocean lies Europe. Look at the outline map of Europe below. Then use it to complete page 91.

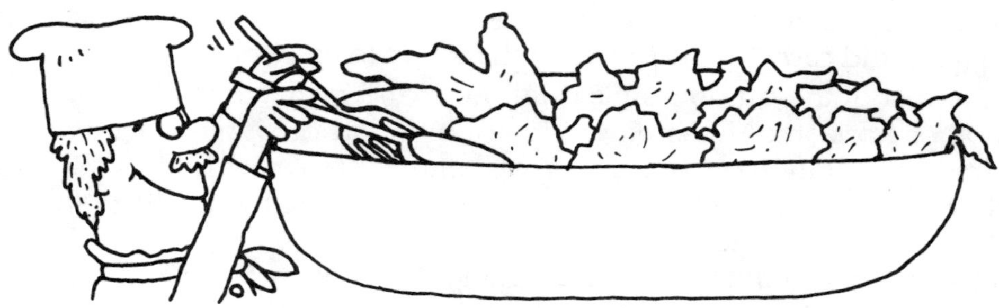

Name ______________________

SCRAMBLED COUNTRIES

To play "Scrambled Countries," first read the statements below. Notice that, in each case, the name of the country is given, but the letters of each name are scrambled.

Using the map on page 90, unscramble the name of each country and write it correctly on the line provided.

1. The country that borders Spain to the north is CREFAN. ______________________
2. The country west of the United Kingdom is ELIRDAN. ______________________
3. South of the Czech Republic is the country of ISATURA. ______________________
4. The country that borders Spain on the west is GLOUPRAT. ______________________
5. The largest country in eastern Europe is ISRUSA. ______________________
6. Two nations that border on Romania are GRANHUY and UGAILARB. ______________________
7. Norway shares a long border with the country of NESWED. ______________________
8. Just to the east of Germany lies DAPLON. ______________________
9. Northwest of the rest of Europe is the island country of CEDANIL. ______________________
10. In the south of Europe is a boot-shaped country called TYLAI. ______________________

Name ____________________

AFRICAN JOURNEY

Cara Van, a member of the Happy Wanderers, will soon be going on a guided bus tour of Africa. She is so excited about her trip that she wants to learn everything she can about that continent before she goes. By studying the two maps below, she has learned 10 facts. See if you can learn the same facts. Look at the maps below. Then use them to complete the statements on page 93.

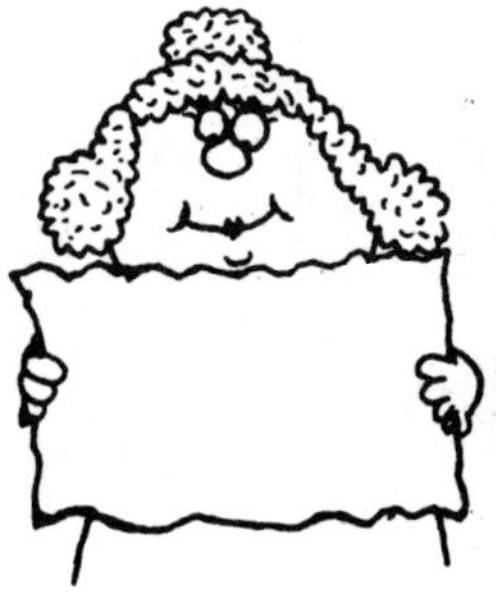

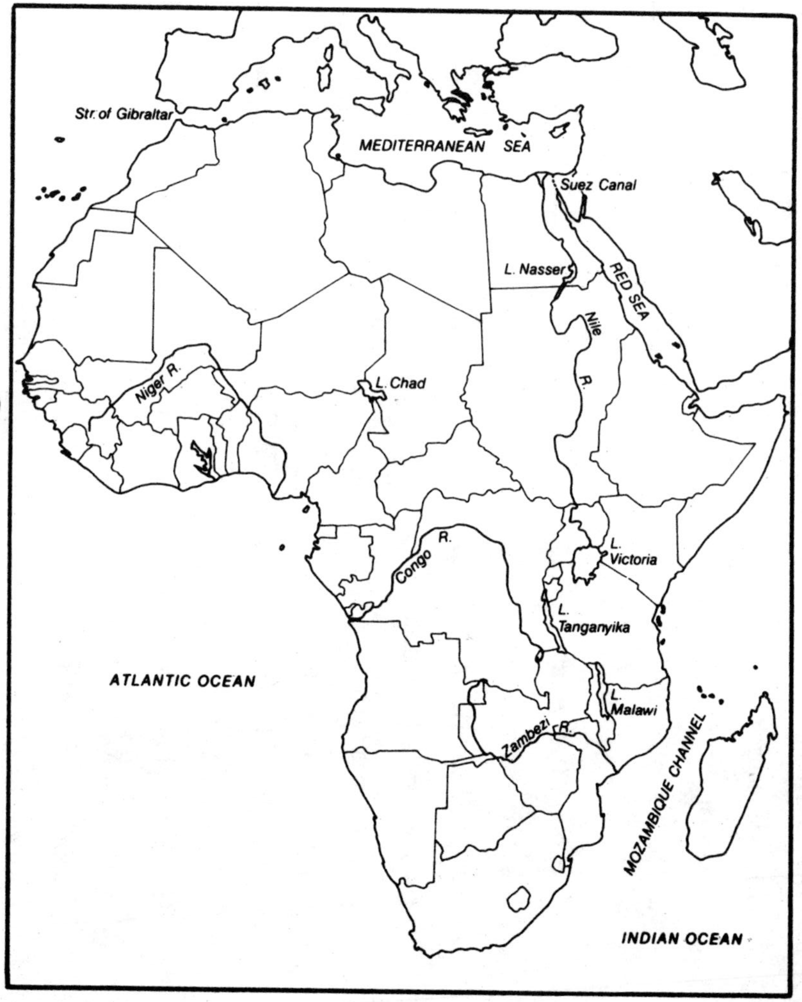

Str. of Gibraltar
MEDITERRANEAN SEA
Suez Canal
L. Nasser
RED SEA
Nile R.
Niger R.
L. Chad
Congo R.
L. Victoria
L. Tanganyika
L. Malawi
Zambezi R.
ATLANTIC OCEAN
MOZAMBIQUE CHANNEL
INDIAN OCEAN

ATLAS MTS.
SAHARA DESERT
ETHIOPIAN HIGHLANDS
NAMIB DESERT
KALAHARI DESERT

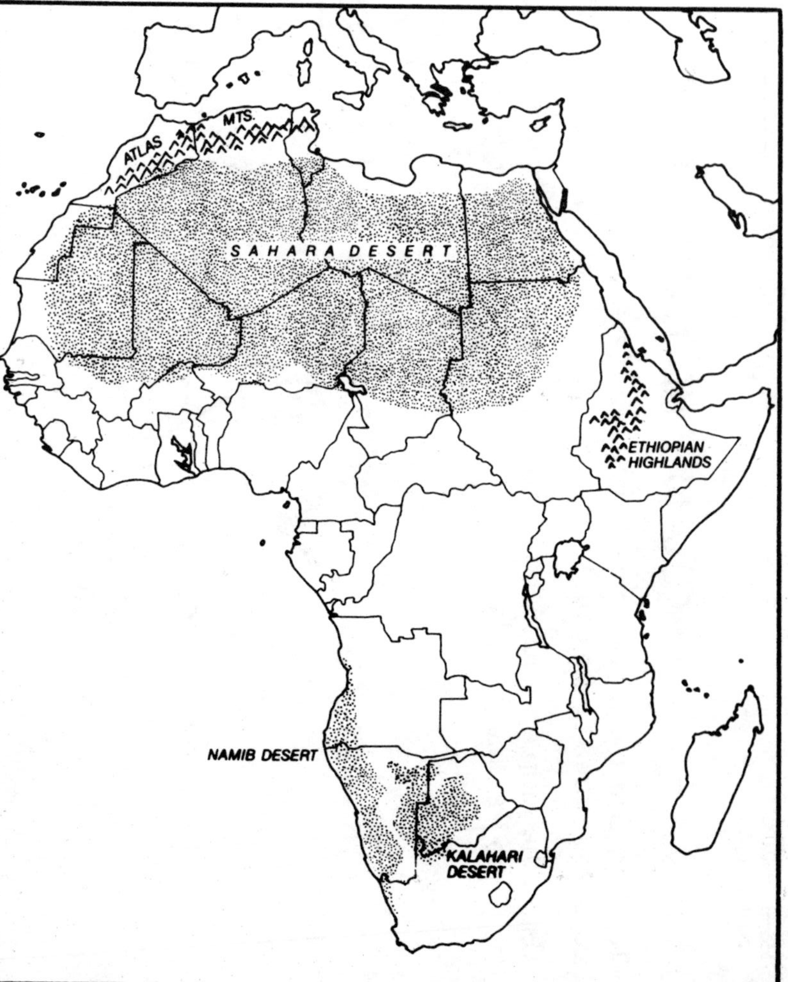

Name ____________________

AFRICAN JOURNEY

Look at the maps on page 92. Then read the facts below. Notice that some words are missing. Use information from the maps to fill in the missing words. Write them on the lines provided.

1. The largest lake in Africa is ____________________ .
2. Four other lakes in Africa are ____________________ , ____________________ , ____________________ , and ____________________ .
3. The longest river in the world is in Africa's northeast section. It is the ____________________ River.
4. Three other long rivers in Africa are the ____________________ , the ____________________ , and the ____________________ .
5. The ____________________ Mountains lie in the northwest part of the African continent.
6. The ____________________ Highlands lie in the eastern part of the African continent.
7. The body of water between the southeast coast of Africa and a large island is called the ____________________ .
8. The largest desert in Africa is called the ____________________ Desert.
9. Two deserts in the southern part of the continent are the Namib Desert and the ____________________ Desert.
10. The waterway connecting the Mediterranean Sea and the Red Sea is the ____________________ Canal.

A DAY IN LONDON

Name ____________________

C. Day Tripper, a member of the Happy Wanderers, is on a whirlwind tour of the capitals of Europe. Today he is in London, the capital of England, with only one day to see the sights. He would like to see as many as he can.

Look at the map below; it shows the central area of London. Notice the map symbols. Then read the Number Key that shows what the numbers on the map stand for. Use this map to complete page 95.

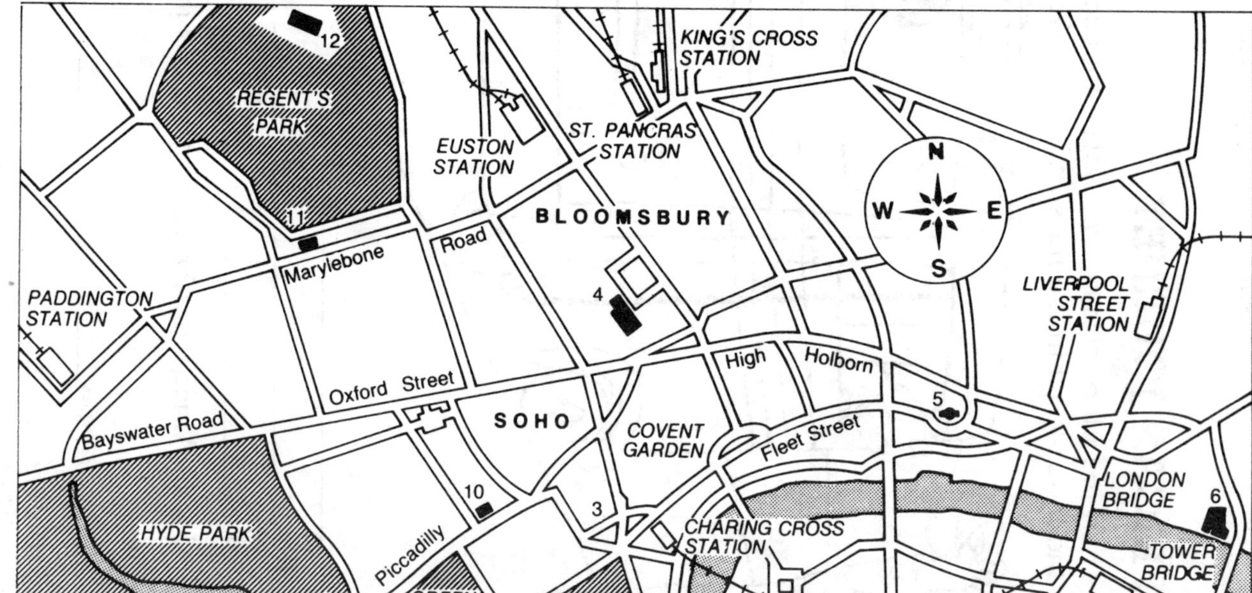

Number Key to London

1. Wellington Museum
2. Buckingham Palace
3. Trafalgar Square
4. British Museum
5. St. Paul's Cathedral
6. Tower of London
7. Imperial War Museum
8. Houses of Parliament
9. Westminster Abbey
10. Royal Academy of Art
11. Madame Tussaud's Wax Museum
12. London Zoo
13. Victoria and Albert Museum
14. Nature and Science Museum

Name ______________________

A DAY IN LONDON

Help C. Day Tripper plan his day in London. Look at the map, map symbols, and Number Key on page 94. Then read C. Day's list of places to see. With a red pencil, mark each place on the map with an **X**. Use this information to answer the questions below. Write your answers on the lines provided. Then with your pencil, draw C. Day's route on the map.

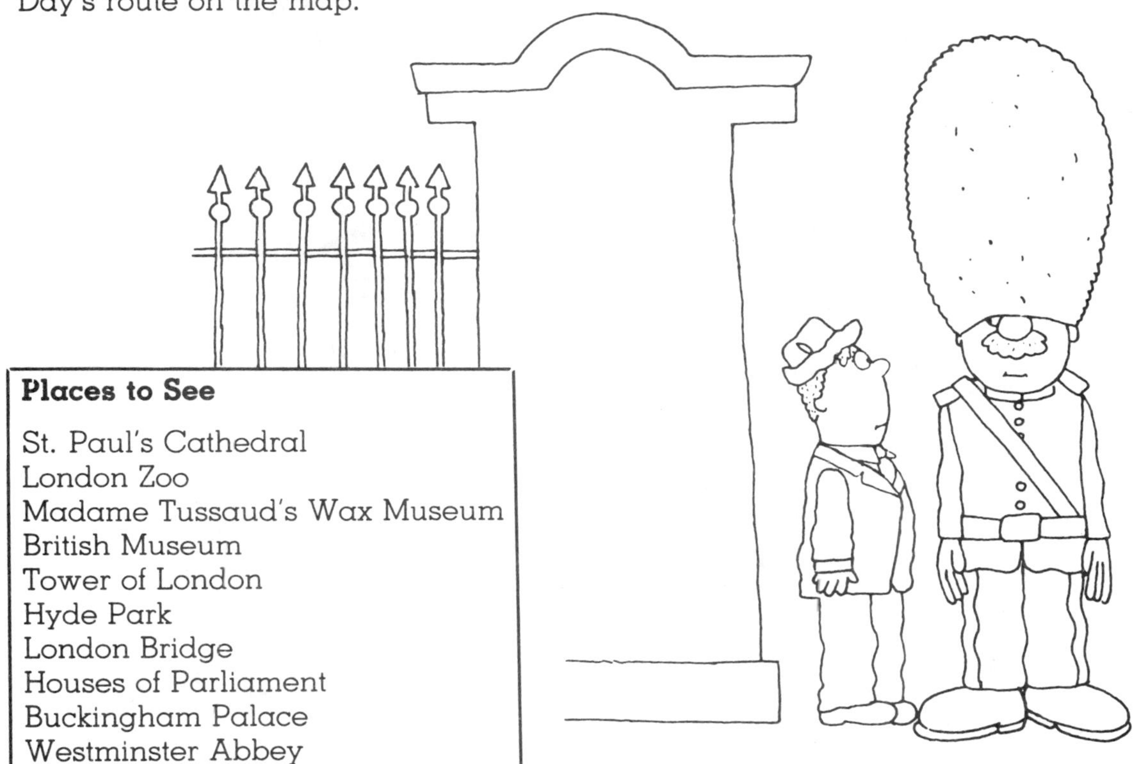

1. C. Day Tripper's hotel is near the Liverpool Street Station. He has decided to see the Tower of London first and then to walk to St. Paul's Cathedral. Which of the other places on his list can he see on the way? ______________________
2. From St. Paul's Cathedral, C. Day will take a bus to Westminster Abbey. There he will also visit another place on his list which is quite close by. What is it? ______________________
3. From Westminster Abbey, C. Day will walk to Hyde Park where he can take a midday rest. On the way he can stop to see the ceremony of the changing of the guard. At which of the places on his list does this take place? ______________________
4. Before strolling through the park to the London Zoo, C. Day will make a stop at Madame Tussaud's Wax Museum. What road is the museum on? ______________________

   ____
5. C. Day will end his tour of London at the British Museum, where he can see the Rosetta stone and the Elgin marbles. In which area of London is this museum located? ______________________

Name ______________________________

THE TASMANIAN DEVILS

Sydney Springs and Adelaide Alice, the owners of a traveling horror show called the Tasmanian Devils, are about to set out on a tour of Australia. They had their route all planned, but some of the goblins in the show ripped up the paper it was written on. You can help them put it back together. First figure out what city the tour sets out from. Read the notes below. On the lines provided, number them to show the correct order. Then look at the map on page 97. Use a red pencil to draw the route on the map.

______ From Cloncurry to Roma

______ From Bourke to Sydney

______ From Halls Creek to Darwin to Alice Springs

______ From Perth to Dongara to Geraldton

______ From Melbourne to Adelaide to Eucla

______ From Geraldton to Onslow

______ From Eucla to Forrest to Perth

______ From Alice Springs to Karumba to Cloncurry

______ From Onslow to Derby to Halls Creek

______ From Roma to Brisbane to Bourke

Name ______________________

THE TASMANIAN DEVILS

Look at the map of Australia below. Use it to complete page 96.

THE KEY TO ASIA

Name ____________________

Look at the map of Asia below. It shows all the countries of the Middle and Far East. Notice the numbers at the top and bottom and the letters along both sides. This is the map key. Use the map and map key to complete page 99.

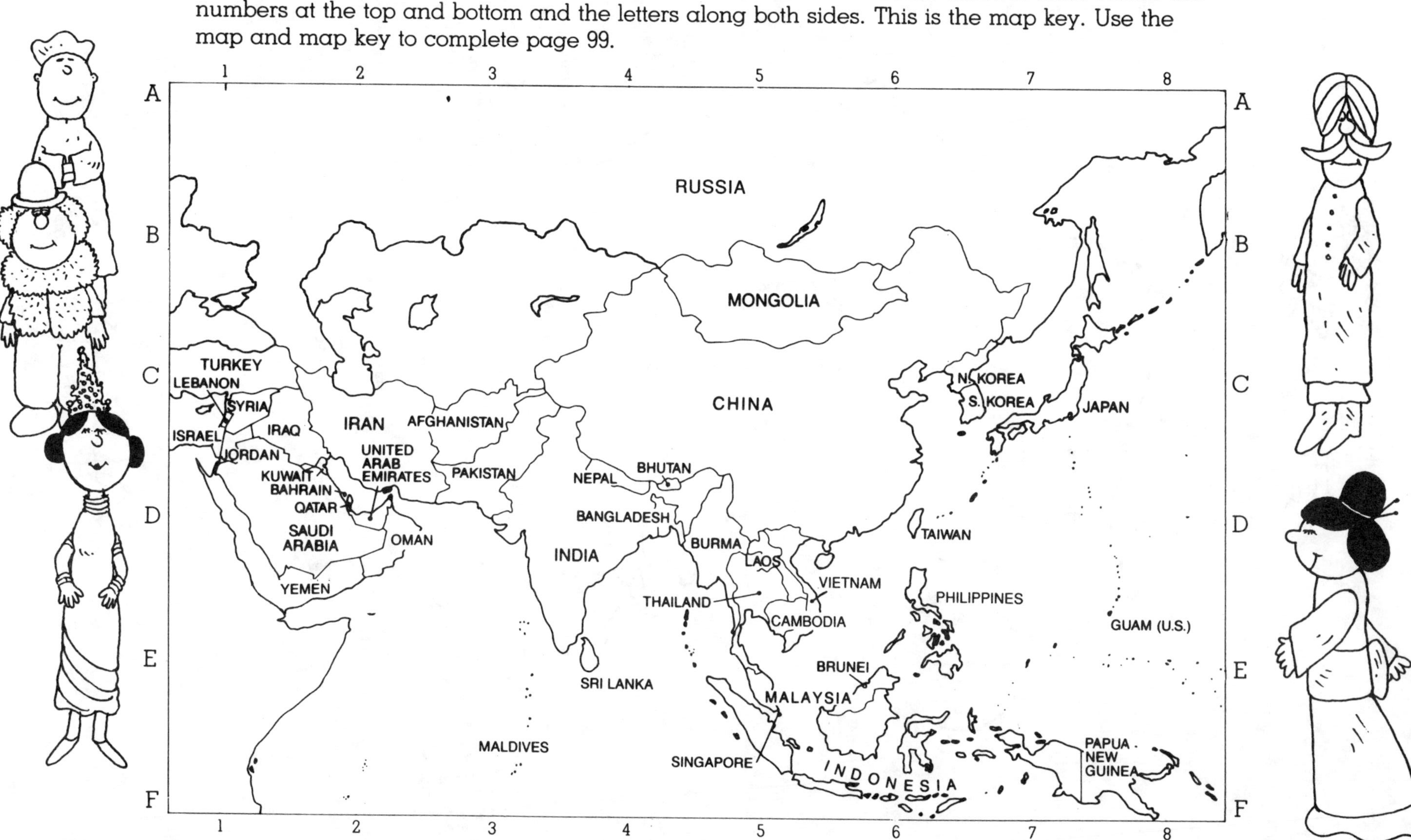

Name ______________________

THE KEY TO ASIA

Look at the map and map key on page 98. (To find out <u>how</u> to use a map key, read the instructions in the box below.) Then read the incomplete atlas index underneath. It lists the countries of Asia in alphabetical order, but the map key letters and numbers are missing for some. On the map, find the missing map key for each country listed. Write your answers on the lines provided.

How to use a map key

Place a finger of one hand on a number and a finger of the other hand on a letter. Then move both fingers in a straight line until they meet. The place you are looking for will be close by.

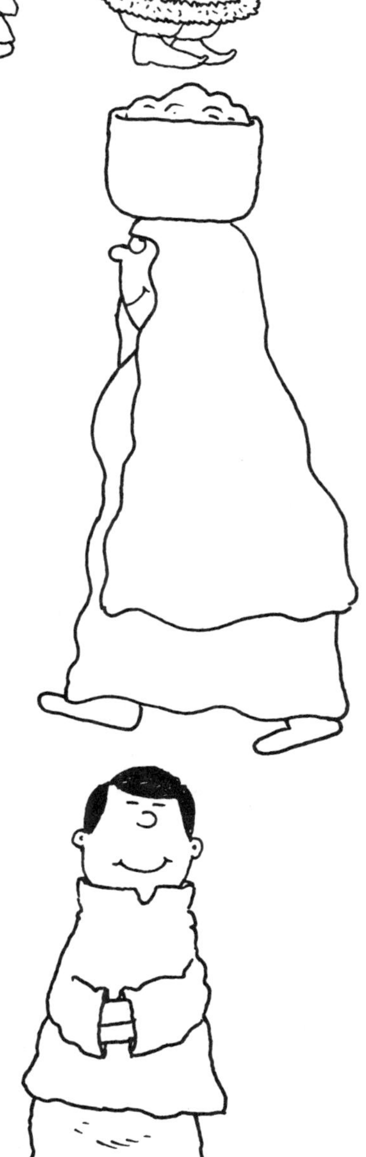

Country	Map Key	Country	Map Key
Afghanistan	C3	Mongolia	B5
Bahrain	______	Nepal	D4
Bangladesh	______	North Korea	C6
Bhutan	D4	Oman	______
Brunei	E6	Pakistan	D3
Burma	D5	Papua New Guinea	F8
Cambodia	______	Yemen	E2
China	C5	Philippines	E6
Guam (U.S.)	E8	Qatar	______
India	D4	Russia	A4
Indonesia	F6	Saudi Arabia	D2
Iran	C2	Singapore	E5
Iraq	C1	South Korea	C7
Israel	C1	Sri Lanka	E4
Japan	______	Syria	______
Jordan	D1	Taiwan	______
Kuwait	D2	Thailand	D5
Laos	______	Turkey	______
Lebanon	C1	United Arab Emirates	______
Malaysia	E5	Vietnam	E5
Maldives	F3		

Name ____________________

BEFORE THE PILGRIMS

Some 13 years before the Pilgrims landed at Plymouth Rock, another group of travelers from England reached the New World. These adventurers sailed across the Atlantic Ocean in three tiny ships. In 1607 they arrived and settled in a colony called Jamestown, in what is now the state of Virginia.

Look at the map below. Notice the lines of latitude and longitude. Then use the instructions on page 101 to trace the route these settlers took.

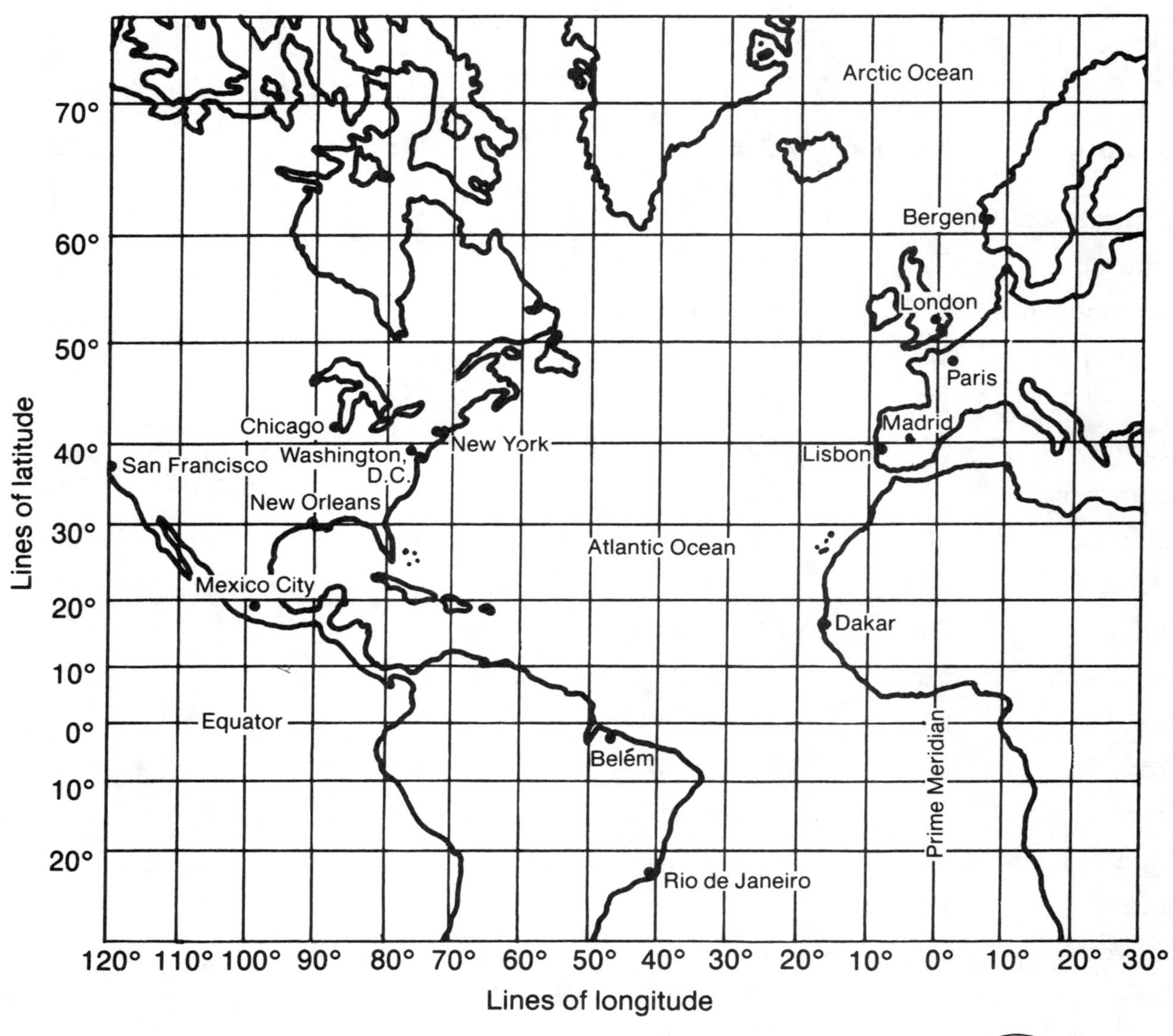

Name ______________________

BEFORE THE PILGRIMS

Read the instructions below. Use them to draw the route of the Jamestown settlers on the map on page 100. If necessary, read the explanation of latitude and longitude on pages 19 and 20. When asked to locate a point in between the degree lines numbered on the map, approximate. For example, if you have to mark 24° N lat., mark a point almost halfway between 20° and 30° N lat.

1. The travelers set sail from the town of Ipswich, England, which is located at 51° N lat., 2° E long. Find this spot and mark it with the letter *I*.
2. Now draw a line down a narrow channel (the English Channel) from Ipswich to the Canary Islands in the Atlantic Ocean off the coast of Africa. These are at 28° N lat., 17° W long. Mark them with a C.
3. Draw a line across the Atlantic Ocean from the Canary Islands to the small island of Martinique (not shown on your map) at 15° N lat., 62° W long. Mark this spot with an *M*.
4. Now continue your line northwest from Martinique to the colony founded by the settlers at Jamestown. This was at approximately 35° N lat., 76° W long. Mark this spot with a *J*.

Answer Sheet for *Around the World*—Section 5

Countries Shape Up—page 86

1. Canada
2. Ireland
3. Zimbabwe
4. Japan
5. Argentina

Make Mine Mexico!—page 87

1. California, Arizona, New Mexico, Texas
2. Rio Grande
3. Mexico; Campeche
4. Sierra Madre (Oriental); Sierra Madre (Occidental)
5. Baja California

Uncle Mac's Map—page 88

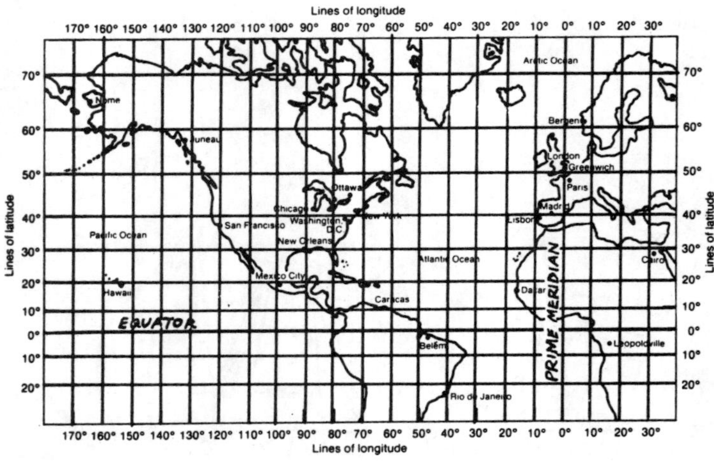

Uncle Mac's Map—page 89

1. New Orleans
2. Nome
3. New York
4. Juneau
5. San Francisco

Scrambled Countries—page 91

1. France
2. Ireland
3. Austria
4. Portugal
5. Russia
6. Hungary; Bulgaria
7. Sweden
8. Poland
9. Iceland
10. Italy

African Journey—page 93

1. Victoria
2. Malawi, Chad, Tanganyika, Nasser
3. Nile
4. Zambezi, Niger, Congo
5. Atlas
6. Ethiopian
7. Mozambique Channel
8. Sahara
9. Kalahari
10. Suez

A Day in London—page 94

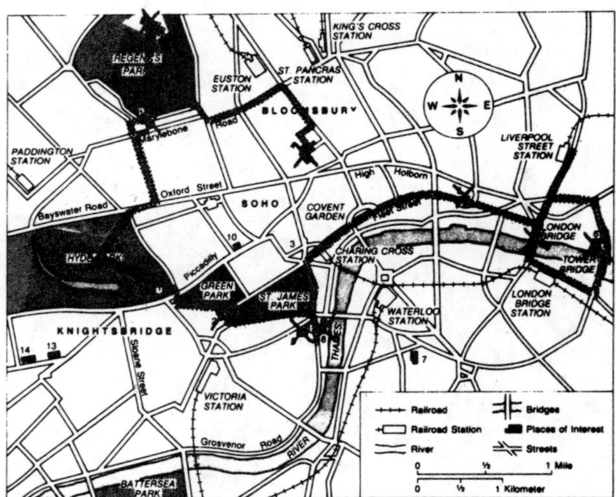

Answer Sheet for *Around the World*—Section 5

A Day in London—page 95

1. London Bridge
2. Houses of Parliament
3. Buckingham Palace
4. Marylebone Road
5. Bloomsbury

The Tasmanian Devils—page 96

The correct sequence is as follows:
8, 10, 6, 3, 1, 4, 2, 7, 5, 9

The Key to Asia—page 99

Country	Map Key	Country	Map Key
Bahrain	D2	Oman	D2
Bangladesh	D4	Qatar	D2
Cambodia	E5	Syria	C1
Japan	C7	Taiwan	D6
Laos	D5	Turkey	C1
		United Arab Emirates	D2

Before the Pilgrims—page 100

The Tasmanian Devils—page 97

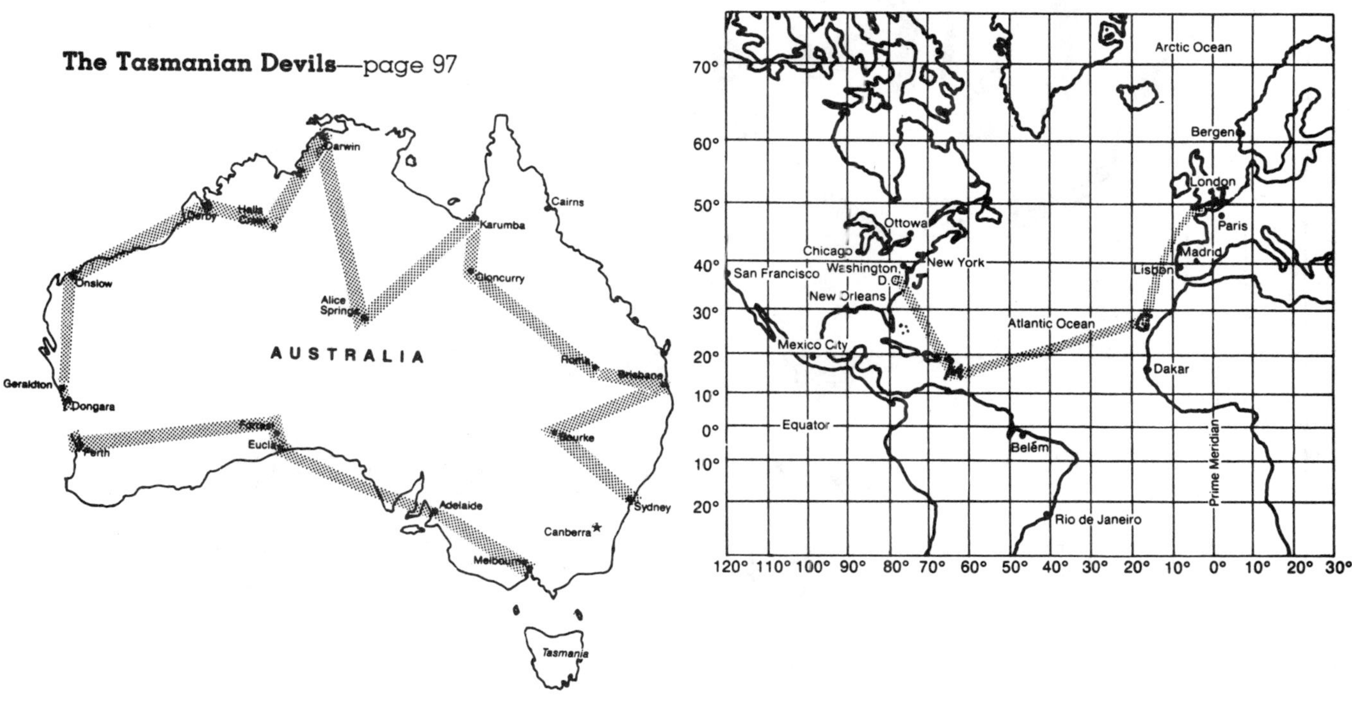

AWARD

HEAR YE! HEAR YE!

____
NAME

is hereby certified as an

A-1, TOPS, SUPER, FIRST-CLASS

MASTER of MAPS

Date ______________________

Teacher's
Signature ______________________

SYMBOLIC SCROLL

AWARDED TO

____

FOR

SUCCESSFULLY GRASPING *Map Symbols*

This pupil has
crossed the)(of knowledge,
climbed the highest skills,
and traveled the ═══ to understanding.

Awarded by ____________________________

on this ____________ day of __________, ____

LATITUDE - LONGITUDE AWARD

Presented to ____________________________

Who has shown a high **DEGREE°** of skill,
PRIME understanding, and ability
without **PARALLEL** in mastering
LATITUDE, LONGITUDE, AND MAP COORDINATES.

Awarded by ____________________________

On this ____________ day of __________, ____

A SPECIAL AWARD
Presented to
WHEN IT COMES
TO
Finding your way around
and
Knowing
where
you are
going
YOU
Really know your
MAPS
and
PLANS
Awarded by
On this
day of